Panaghiótis Chrístou - Katharini Papastamatis

GODS AND

GREEK MYTHOLOGY

THE TROJAN WAR, THE ODYSSEY, AND THE AENEID

Colossal head of Zeus. Part of an enormous marble statue of Zeus enthroned, discovered at Aegira in Achaea. Generally identified with the work by the Athenian sculptor Eucles recorded at Aegira in the 2nd century AD by Pausanias. Athens, National Archaeological Museum.

Tel. +39 055 576841 - Fax +39 055 5000766
E-mail: bonechi@bonechi.it Internet: www.bonechi.it www.bonechi.com

Publication created and designed by Casa Editrice Bonechi
Editorial management: Giovanna Magi
Picture research: Giovanna Magi, Francesco Giannoni
Graphic design, layout, and make up: Sonia Gottardo
Cover: Sonia Gottardo
Editing and text boxes: Patrizia Fabbri
Text: Panaghiótis Chrístou, Katharini Papastamatis
Translation: Heather Mackay Roberts, Paula Boomsliter
Illustrations: Alessandro Bartolozzi *(pages 116a, 118)*, Alessandra Chiarlo *(pages 59, 61, 62, 63, 112a, 136a, 137b)*, Linda Imposimato *(pages 56, 70, 72, 73, 94b, 109b, 131a)*.

Printed in Italy by Centro Stampa Editoriale Bonechi.

The majority of the photographs are property of the Casa Editrice Bonechi *Archives.*
Other photographs were provided by
Cassa di Risparmio di Firenze *(by permission): page 83a;*
G. Dagli Orti: *pages 10, 11b, 12, 14, 18b, 22-24, 26b, 30, 34, 36, 37, 40, 41b, 42a, 44, 47, 48, 50a, 53, 56a, 57b, 60, 64a, 67, 69, 71, 78, 79, 84a, 87-91, 95, 96, 97b, 98, 99, 101, 102b, 103, 105, 107, 108, 111, 112b, 113, 114ac, 115, 126b, 129, 133, 136b, 138-139, 142a;*
Kunsthistorisches Museum: *pages 18a, 35a, 54b, 82a, 106;*
Vatican Museums (A. Bracchetti, P. Zigrossi): *pages 11a, 140;*
Rethymnon Archaeological Museum: *page 76a;*
Scala Group: *pages 4-5, 7-9, 17, 42b, 50b, 52, 77, 80, 86, 114b, 123, 125a, 127, 130, 132.*

ISBN 88-476-0886-4

* * *

INTRODUCTION

Throughout man's long history, all peoples, no matter how sophisticated their society, have felt the need to create sets of myths and legends to justify, explain, and interpret the meaning of nature's mysteries and to understand the forces behind life: from atmospheric phenomena to the source of a spring, from the infinite variety and shades of plant life to the destructive fury of an earthquake; to the hidden subtleties of the human psyche and spirit. The fervid and creative imagination of the people of Greece, constantly enriched by cultural interchange and open to the influx of stimuli from the entire Mediterranean area, developed a rationalized and detailed corpus of myths that followed in logical progression from the ancient narrated sagas and was organized by clearly delineated genealogies.

Yet it must be remembered that this "system" is in no way unequivocal. Quite the contrary. There exist many versions of the same myths, conditioned by the city or geographical area in which they developed, by the period in which they were created, and by the cultural milieus in which they were refined and fleshed out (just think of the variations that may be introduced to a myth in relation to its role in religious practice, as a metaphor of philosophical thought, or through the revitalizing effects of theatrical representation.) Another key element in mythical tradition is the role played by the modes in which the myths have been transmitted. Many are known to us only from written sources (and this work clearly offers only a limited selection from the numerous possible versions); we know of others only from archaeological sources: scenes illustrated on vases, in bronzes, in reliefs, on sarcophagi, and in decorative architectural elements from all ages.

To all this, we must add the difficulties encountered by modern-day interpreters in reading these stories correctly after thousands of years. The problems do not stop with those inherent to the narrative and its immediate meaning but frequently continue when the interpreter delves beyond the story into the hidden symbolic meaning implied by a mythological presentation. Nor must we forget that even in ancient times the same myth could take on different shades of meaning and relative weights according to place—Greece, Magna Graecia, or Etruria—even though it was formulated in the same formal language everywhere.

It is also vital to remember that all the while a lively oral tradition continued, shaping and changing the myths and adapting them to changing circumstances.

This composite, eclectic matrix of diversified elements and forms resulted in the nearly spontaneous generation of mythical sagas that

were in practice universal but nonetheless different in every region of the Greek world, especially in those dominated by supreme cultural centers. Athens' cultural hegemony extended to Attica and the surrounding regions, Corinth's to the northeastern Peloponnese, and Sparta's to Lacedaemon and the southern Peloponnese.
The myths narrated here were shaped in these three areas of cultural influence. It must not be forgotten, however, that in the more remote or isolated areas different versions developed, and that over time some of the variants assumed greater importance than the original "official" versions.
Another warning. Greek mythology should not be confused with ancient Greek religion, even though the two are inextricably linked. The myths form the basis of religious beliefs of that people, with its feasts, its established practices, and its ceremonial rites both public and private. In this lies the fundamental difference: mythology was subject to change and development, religion was the immutable foundation.
The Greek myths were adopted, adapted, and transmitted by the Romans and interpreted by medieval scholars before the Renaissance and Humanism. They were reread and reinterpreted by Neoclassicism and Romanticism and endure even in the peculiar metaphysical interpretations of modern art. In short, over time the values expressed by the figures created by ancient Greek mythology and the concepts they came to represent have been gradually but thoroughly absorbed by all the cultures of the western world.
There is, in fact, no country in the western world where the name of Odysseus (Ulysses) fails to strike a particular chord: his cunning is proverbial, as is his yearning for his homeland; the immortal image of his sovereign anxiety weaves through James Joyce's 20th century literary masterpiece that bears the hero's name. Who does not know of the dramatic unfolding of the destiny of the royal family of Thebes—or at least the "Oedipus complex" named after its principal player by Sigmund Freud? And what of the strength of Heracles (Hercules), the fidelity of Penelope, Antigone's love for her brother, the mutual loyalty of Achilles and Patrocles, the beauty of Aphrodite, the power of Eros, or the impartiality of Zeus?

Zeus, Father of the Gods, enthroned and holding his scepter, presides over the assembly of the gods on Mount Olympus. Fresco by Luigi Sabatelli (1772-1850) in the central tondo in the ceiling of the Sala dell'Iliade. Florence, Palazzo Pitti.
Many gods in the crowded gathering are clearly recognizable. To the left of the throne is Ganymede, the handsome cup-bearer, and the superb Athena at whose feet sits majestic Poseidon; then the unmistakable Hermes, behind Hephaestus, and the splendid Aphrodite, languidly embracing Eros; the three Graces, with dreamy expressions, and behind them Dionysus, crowned as always with vines and grapes and flanked by his love, Ariadne; and Ares, warlike in his dress and attitude, and the satyr-like Pan, his intense glance of complicity fixed on the solar Demeter, her tresses adorned with light blond spikes of grain.
In the representation of the great assembly of the gods, Eos, to Zeus' right, floats throwing flowers above the vexed Hera, who seems to be giving a scolding look to her majestic husband, alongside whom is the ever-present eagle. At Hera's feet is a darkling Hades, with a subdued Persephone and the three-headed dog Cerberus. Next, beside an elegant peacock, an animal sacred to Hera, are the divine twins Apollo and the virginal Artemis, whose hair shines with the pure candor of a crescent moon. Behind the sons of Leto, Asclepias observes the serpent that has always been his symbol as he stands next to Hestia, goddess of the domestic hearth. Lower down, a gigantic Heracles enveloped in the lion's skin speaks with a gentle Hebe. And meanwhile, at the center of the scene, the impenetrable, mysterious Moirai continue to spin the threads of destiny and thus inexorably pattern the fates of men and the course of events in the world.

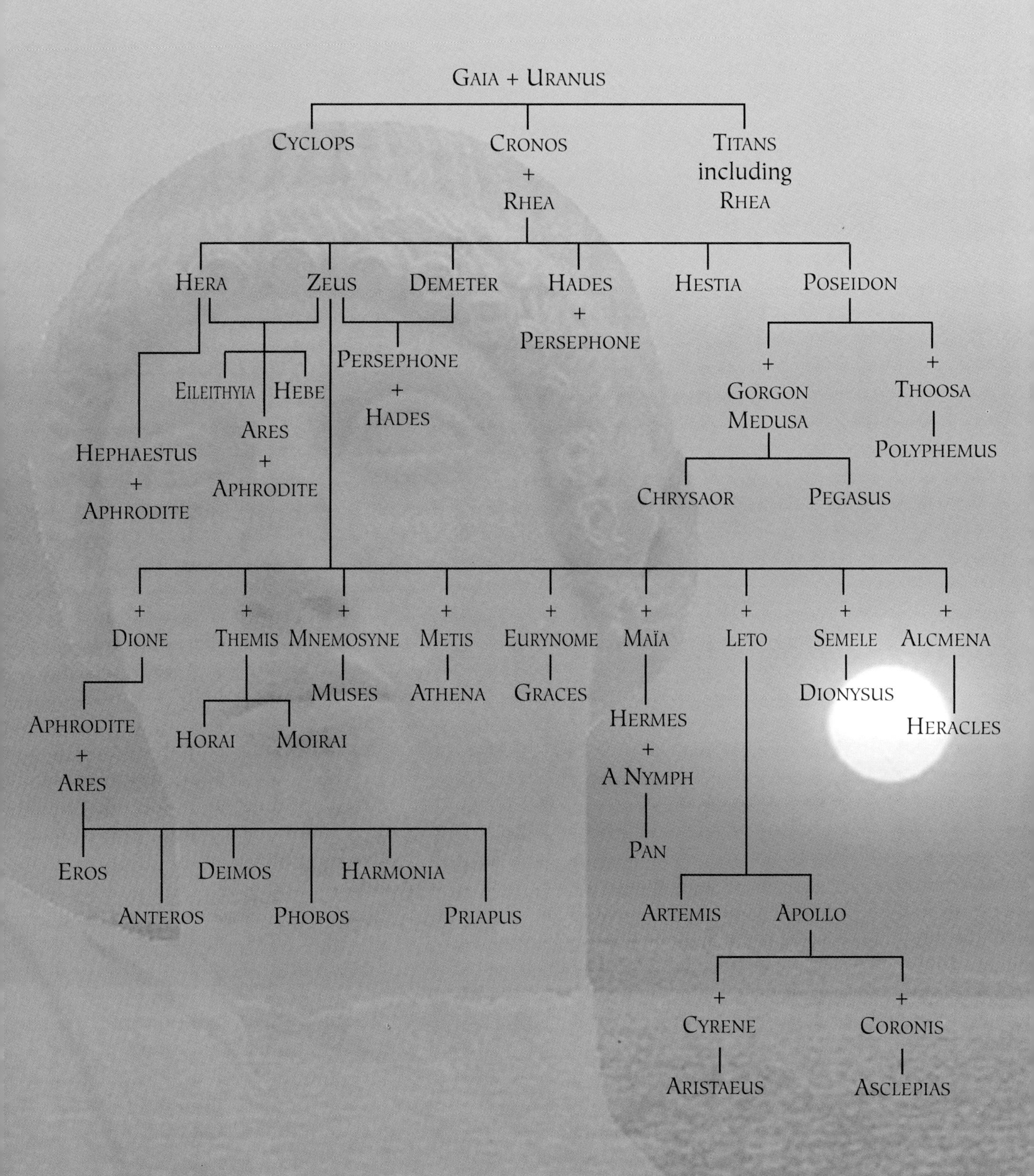
GAIA + URANUS
CYCLOPS
CRONOS
+
RHEA
TITANS
including
RHEA
HERA
ZEUS
DEMETER
HADES
+
PERSEPHONE
HESTIA
POSEIDON
EILEITHYIA
HEBE
PERSEPHONE
+
HADES
+
GORGON
MEDUSA
+
THOOSA
ARES
+
APHRODITE
HEPHAESTUS
+
APHRODITE
POLYPHEMUS
CHRYSAOR
PEGASUS
+
DIONE
+
THEMIS
+
MNEMOSYNE
+
METIS
+
EURYNOME
+
MAÏA
+
LETO
+
SEMELE
+
ALCMENA
MUSES
ATHENA
GRACES
DIONYSUS
APHRODITE
+
ARES
HORAI
MOIRAI
HERMES
+
A NYMPH
HERACLES
PAN
EROS
DEIMOS
HARMONIA
ANTEROS
PHOBOS
PRIAPUS
ARTEMIS
APOLLO
+
CYRENE
+
CORONIS
ARISTAEUS
ASCLEPIAS

CHAPTER I

THE PRE-OLYMPIAN GODS

Mother Earth and Uranus

Mother Earth (or Gaia) was born out of Chaos, the unbounded emptiness of the Universe, and she was immediately followed by Eros, Love. It was Gaia, the primordial element from which the gods descended, who alone generated Pontus (the Sea) and Uranus (the Sky).
The union between Gaia and Uranus—the immensity of the Sky made him alone capable of covering the Earth—was extremely fruitful; among their progeny were the twelve Titans, six male and six female, and the Cyclops'. When Gaia, tired of her excessive fertility, implored her offspring to free her from the brutal embrace of Uranus, they all refused except her last-born, Cronos (Time), who, armed with a sickle, castrated his father and threw his testicles into the sea. The drops of blood falling to the Earth from the mutilation of Uranus gave birth to the Erinyes (Furies), the Giants, and the Nymphs of the Ash-trees (Meliads). The sickle thrown into the sea is traditionally identified with the island of Corfu, home of the magical sea-faring Phaeacians, who are said to have sprung from the blood of Uranus.

Cronos and Rhea: the Birth of the Gods

Cronos, after liberating Mother Earth and confining all his brothers to Tartarus (the lowest region of the Earth, sited even below the Underworld), assumed power and married Rhea, one of his Titan sisters.
Since it had been prophesied that Cronos would be overthrown by one of his offspring, he devoured each of them at birth: Hestia, Demeter, Hera, Hades, and Poseidon.
Rhea's maternal instinct saved Zeus from Cronos' brutality. To protect her sixth child, she took refuge in Crete where in the dead of night and secretly she gave birth to the infant god in a cave on Mount Ida. To allay the suspicions of Cronos she gave him a large stone to eat, wrapped in a blanket. Zeus grew rapidly, fed on the miraculous milk of the goat Amalthea, while the Curetes and the Corybantes (benevolent spirits) rattled their spears on their shields to conceal the cries of the child from the vengeful Cronos.

The 16th century Allegory of the Earth *by Giorgio Vasari and Cristoforo Gherardi.* Florence, Palazzo Vecchio, Room of the Elements.

Zeus and the Titanomachy: the Olympian Pantheon

When he reached manhood, Zeus indeed sought to overthrow his father. He asked advice of Metis (Prudence), who gave him an emetic potion to administer to Cronos so that he would disgorge his other children. His liberated brothers then joined him in battle against Cronos who, in the meantime, had freed his own brothers from Tartarus. The ensuing ten-year war (the "Battle of the Gods and Titans" or Titanomachy) ended with the victory of Zeus and his brothers, the Olympian gods. Cronos and the Titans were chased from the heavens and forced to face the merciless punishment of Zeus: the Titan Atlas, for example, was condemned to hold up the firmament for all eternity. After their victory the gods divided power among themselves by lot: Hades was given the Underworld and a magic helmet that made him invisible; Poseidon was allotted the Sea and a trident to shake the earth and waters; Zeus held the heavens with the thunder and lightning forged by the Cyclops' and predominated over the entire Universe.

The Gigantomachy: the Definitive Establishment of Order

The division of power, nevertheless, did not ensure peace for very long: when Gaia learned that her sons the Titans had once again been confined to the darkness of Tartarus, she formed an alliance with the Giants born of the drops of blood shed by Uranus after his castration by Cronos. The Olympian gods thus found themselves facing the menacing aggression of enormous beings of terrifying appearance and overpowering strength, with bristly hair and serpent legs. All the Olympian gods joined in the battle, led by Zeus with his powerful thunderbolt and the protection of the aegis, the magical skin of the goat Amalthea who had nourished him as an infant. Athena, Zeus's favorite daughter and a direct emanation of the god himself, having emerged fully armed from his head, also fought under the protection of the aegis—which in her case was adorned with the terrible Gorgon's head, given to her by Perseus as a sign of his gratitude for goddess' aid in decapitating the monster. In their battle against the Giants, the Olympians gods had by way of exception an ally of great strength and prowess: Heracles, received on Olympus by the gods in recognition his virtues and the ability he had shown in performing a series of twelve arduous labors. His involvement was also the fulfilment of the prophecy that the Giants could be defeated only if attacked simultaneously by a god and a mortal—which Heracles was.

The Titan Atlas was condemned to bear the weight of the sky for all eternity as punishment for having rebelled against Zeus. Marble Roman statue (2nd century AD), known as the Farnese Atlas. Naples, National Archaeological Museum.

The Creation of Man

Once the original Chaos was replaced by divine order, with the gods in the heavens and the opposing brute forces confined to the Underworld, Zeus populated the Earth with a variety of beings. He then ordered two of his cousins descended from the Titans, Epimetheus and Prometheus, to distribute the gifts of the gods among all the creatures of the Earth.
Epimetheus began by sharing out the gifts of the gods among animals and plants: beauty to one species and strength to another, agility to the smaller beings, cunning to those without other defenses, and intelligence to the physically weak.
But he proved to be rather clumsy distributor, since he left the human race until last and, what's more, ran out of gifts to bestow. Mankind thus appeared condemned to remain naked, weak, and devoid of natural defenses. But Epimetheus' brother Prometheus (often considered the major benefactor of man and in some later traditions also his creator, having modeled him out of clay) intervened to restore balance by reserving certain gifts for humankind—and in his desire to assist man even went so far as to deceive Zeus. During a solemn sacrifice, he divided an ox into two parts, one with the meat and innards covered by the skin; the other with the bones alone concealed in the white fat. Then he asked Zeus to choose his portion, that the other might be left to the men. The Father of the Gods selected the fatty part, but when he discovered that all it contained were bare bones his anger was so great that he punished mankind by withdrawing one of their most precious gifts, fire. Once again, Prometheus came to man's aid. Having stolen several flames from the wheel of the Sun (or, according to other versions, from the furnace of Hephaestus), he restored fire and the hope of survival to the human race. Zeus then took his vengeance. Prometheus was chained to a mountain in the Caucasus, where the eagle of Zeus devoured his liver by day; each night it regrew, only to be devoured again. He was freed some thirty years later by Heracles, who killed the ferocious eagle. To man, instead, Zeus sent **Pandora**, the first woman, modeled with the help of all the gods.

Pandora

When the gods of Olympus joined forces to create Pandora, they were nothing less than prodigal in their extravagance. And thus the young woman, as her very name suggests (Pandora = "she with all the gifts") was endowed with countless qualities: beauty, grace, manual dexterity, and persuasion; but the spiteful Hermes also touched her heart with deceit and guile. Zeus sent her as a gift to Epimetheus, who, forgetting his brother Prometheus' advice to be wary of Zeus and his gifts, was won over by her great beauty and married her. Before sending her to Earth, however, Zeus had given her a jar containing all wickedness. No sooner had Pandora arrived, and despite the warnings and strictures placed on her by Epimetheus, than her consuming curiosity won out and she opened the jar: thus, all the evil it contained spread among mankind. Another tradition describes the vase as containing every kind of goodness, which flew out when Pandora lifted the lid; she replaced it just in time to prevent Hope from escaping from the bottom.

The Titan Prometheus, punished by Zeus for having deceived him and helping man, was imprisoned in the mountains of the Caucasus where the eagle of Zeus daily devoured his liver. Opposite him stands the Titan Atlas, forced to support the weight of the heavens. Laconian cup decorated by the Arkesilas Painter (ca. 550 BC). Rome, Vatican Museums.

The Battle of the Gods and Giants: in the foreground, Hera, the mother of the gods, fights the enemy. Detail of the frieze on the north side of the Siphnian Treasury, a votive building with sculpted decoration dedicated in about 525 BC by the inhabitants of the island of Siphnos to the sanctuary of the Pythian Apollo at Delphi. Delphi, Archaeological Museum.

Deucalion and Pyrrha

Infuriated by brutal and corrupt mankind, Zeus decided to exterminate all men by drowning them in a tremendous flood. All men, that is, except Deucalion, son of Prometheus, and his wife Pyrrha, daughter of Epimetheus and therefore also his cousin, the only two good and just humans.
To ensure their salvation, the Father of the Gods instructed the couple to build a wooden ark that floated on the flood waters that raged over the Earth for nine days and nine nights. When the waters began to recede, they made land on the mountain peaks of Thessaly, where, according to tradition, they were welcomed by Hermes sent by Zeus to grant them one unconditional wish. Deucalion and Pyrrha requested the company of other human creatures so as not to pass the rest of their lives in total solitude. Zeus then ordered them to throw the bones of their mother over their shoulders. The suggestion of such an impious act struck terror into the heart of Pyrrha, but Deucalion interpreted the words correctly and understood that Zeus referred to stones, the "bones" of Mother Earth (Gaia). The stones tossed by Deucalion generated men and those cast by Pyrrha women, and so the Earth was repopulated.

The Flood

The Flood in the ceiling fresco of the Sistine Chapel, painted by the able hand of Michelangelo. Vatican City, Rome.

The traditions of all the ancient cultures transmit the memory of a devastating cataclysm, a "universal" deluge. Recent archaeological discoveries tend to confirm that in about the 4th millennium BC the area of Lower Mesopotamia, in that historical era the cradle of one of the world's most advanced civilizations, was plausibly inundated. But the story of what is universally called the Flood, with its tragic death toll and the utter destruction it wreaked, also appears in Indian culture with the story of Manu, among the Scandinavians, and in the folklore of Southeast Asia; the most famous of these stories is undoubtedly the Biblical narration of the trials of Noah and his ark, which in so many details so closely parallel the tribulations of Utnapishtim, the man who according to Babylonian tradition (the myth of Gilgamish) subtracted his family and examples of all the species of animals and plants existing on earth from the fury of the waters. Deucalion and Pyrrha, the survivors of Greek mythology, are but another exhibit in this gallery of characters, the witnesses called to transmit to future generations the memory of one of the most terrifying cataclysms ever to have invested the planet.

Poseidon, Ares, and Hermes in battle against the Giants, who are already succumbing to the superior strength of the gods. Attic red-figure pelike painted by an artist near the Pronomos Painter (ca. 400 BC). Athens, National Archaeological Museum.

For mankind, she proved to be the font of all evil.
Despite the gifts granted them by the gods and the aid of Prometheus, as it multiplied and progressed the human race failed to win favor with Zeus. The supreme god, in fact, was so appalled by human passions and vices that he thought it best to destroy the man outright by sending a devastating universal **flood**. Thus begins the story of **Deucalion and Pyrrha**, the only two good and just people to be found on all the Earth and for this reason the only two believed by Zeus to be worthy of salvation. They became the progenitors of a new human race.

CHAPTER II

THE GODS OF OLYMPUS

Zeus, the Father of the Gods

The gods of the Greek pantheon were splendid in their illuminated magnificence, omnipotent in their divine faculties, and yet nevertheless prey to the same passions and weaknesses as the mortals they governed. Nor were their dealings with each other and with men without a certain capriciousness. Their sometimes epic, sometimes dramatic, sometimes whimsical doings, especially those of the first generations of gods, fully reflect the slow and labored process of myth-making and the formation of a mythological corpus. The sources are unanimous in citing **Mount Olympus**, on the border between Macedonia and Thessaly, as the dwelling-place of the Greek gods, and Olympus was not long in becoming the symbol par excellence of a celestial abode.

The most famous divine couple of classical antiquity: Zeus and Hera, who together dominated the Greek Pantheon. The Father of the Gods is crowned by Victory, assisted by Mercury who is ready to take flight to communicate orders from Zeus. Drawing after a red-figure Attic hydria (ca. 440 BC). Leiden (Netherlands), Leiden Museum of Antiquities.

Born of Cronos and Rhea, nourished by the magical goat Amalthea, protected by Nymphs and Corybantes, and come to wield absolute power after his defeat of the Giants and Titans, Zeus was the god of mortals and reigned supreme over the other immortals. He was, essentially, the god of light, of thunder, and of lightning—and thus of all the celestial manifestations—and expressed his power through his attributes: lightning, a source of illumination but also capable of destruction; the scepter, symbol of his regality; the eagle, his messenger; the aegis, the skin of the goat Amalthea, as impenetrable as the strongest armor. With these symbols to affirm his power, Zeus ruled as guarantor of the established order, dispenser of justice, and repository of regal power and the social hierarchy: all prerogatives he asserted not only over men but also over the entire gathering of the gods.
From the union of Zeus and Hera, his wife and sister, were born Ares, the god of war, Eileithyia, the goddess of childbirth, capable of multiplying herself as the occasion demanded, and Hebe, the goddess of youth. Zeus's innumerable couplings with other females, both divine and human, gave birth to all the other gods, the demigods, and illustrious heroes of ancient Greece.

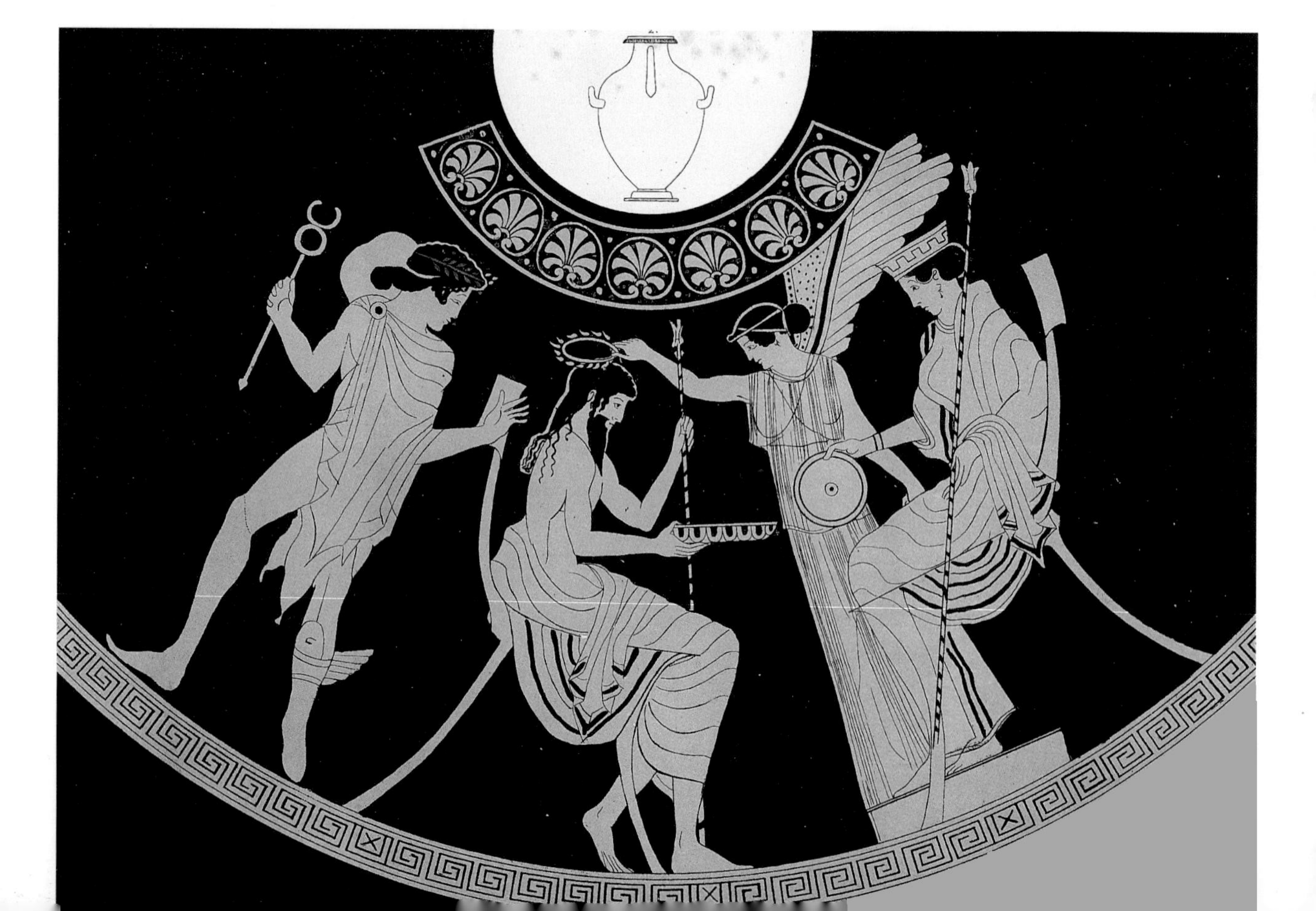

Left, the three Graces as painted in oil on copper by Poppi (Francesco Morandini) in 1571. Florence, Uffizi.

Themis, goddess of justice and chronologically the second wife of Zeus—and his chief adviser. Marble statue by Chairestratos, son of Chairedemos (ca. 280 BC) for the temple of Themis at Ramnous in Attica. Athens, National Archaeological Museum.

The Transformations and Amorous Exploits of Zeus

The most important of Zeus's divine loves was undoubtedly Metis, the goddess of prudence, who was also his first wife in chronological terms. After several vain attempts to escape the advances of Zeus and having to this end assumed the most disparate forms, Metis was finally compelled to surrender to him. It was from their union that Athena was conceived.
But since Gaia (Earth) had prophesied that Metis would bear a daughter whose son would eventually overthrow Zeus, the Father of the Gods swallowed Metis to continue the gestation of their child himself.
In the meantime, Zeus' wife Hera, jealous of her husband's extra-marital exploits and of his capacity

to manage a typically womanly undertaking like childbirth, generated a son unfertilized by any male: Hephaestus, the god of fire. When the appointed time came, it was this "half-brother" of Zeus' child who split open the father's head with his axe to allow Athena to emerge, already fully armed. Equally famous and celebrated is the union between Zeus and Leto, from which were born Apollo, the god of light, and Artemis, the goddess of the hunt. As Leto's time of birth approached, the green-eyed Hera punished Leto by forcing her to wander the world: for fear of Hera's anger, no land "whether on terra firma or at sea" would receive Leto. The only place that did nor fall under this definition was the island of Delos at the center of the Aegean, then a floating island and difficult to reach on account of the strong underwater currents in the area. It was here, neither strictly at sea nor on truly solid ground, that Leto gave birth to the most celebrated of the divine twins. As a sign of her gratitude, Delos was secured to the seabed by the four columns that have anchored it ever since. Later, the most important of all the sanctuaries dedicated to Apollo was established on the island.
Dione, the daughter of Uranus (or perhaps of Oceanus: tradition conflicts here) bore Zeus' daughter Aphrodite, the goddess of love. Dione is in fact the feminine of the name Zeus and like "Zeus" signifies "god of the luminous heavens." Since she was also the goddess of water and of the springs whence oracles were received, Dione was often associated with Oceanus, the father of all flowing waters and the personification of that vital element. From his union with another of his sisters, Demeter, the goddess of grain and of cultivation, Zeus fathered Persephone (also known as Core, "the Maiden"), future goddess of the underworld and companion to Hades. Themis, the goddess of justice and of eternal law, in addition to her role as counselor to Zeus (it was she who suggested that he protect himself with the aegis, the skin of the goat Amalthea, during the battle against the Giants) and to the other gods (she taught Apollo the art of divination), was also one of the wives of the Father of the Gods—the second in chronological order. Their union generated numerous progeny, including the three Horai, the goddesses of the seasons (associated with the hours of the day only in later traditions), and the three Moirai, the Fates (long life, happiness, fortune, etc.). The latter three sisters operated according to an inflexible law which not even the gods could transgress: they regulated the length of every man's life with a thread that was spun by the first, drawn off by the second, and cut by the third at the final fatal hour.

Zeus, infatuated with the beautiful Ganymede, abducts him while he is tending her father's herds in the mountains of the Troas and carries him off in flight to Olympus. Terracotta group from a temple in Olympia (ca. 480-470 BC). Olympia, Archaeological Museum.

Right, clear streams run down the green slopes of Mount Olympus. In Homer's poetic description the mountain is "high and covered in snows," but its heights are often hidden in a dense crown of clouds.

Olympus

Mount Olympus, in Thessaly, is a high, steeply-sloped mountain whose eternal snow cap separates the pure blue of the sky from the intense green of the pines and olives that grow on its sides and is echoed in the white foam of the sea that washes its foot. Perhaps on account of its ethereal appearance, since indeed the mountain seems to be detached from any terrestrial moorings, the Greeks saw its cloud-shrouded peak as the seat of the pantheon, the mythical assembly of the gods enlivened by the company of the Graces and the Muses. From Olympus, on orders imparted by the almighty Zeus (who assumed the epithet "Olympian"), the gods governed the destinies of the men who were born, lived, and died on Earth. Man's existence was entirely subject to the decisions (not always equitable) of the gods, who at times aided Man, at times defended him with merciful compassion, and at others inexorably overpowered him, but who were never really touched by human doings, in their "olympian" detachment from all things earthly. A mountain raised to the rank of symbol—and over time a universal symbol—of a transmundane serenity and imperturbability the attainment of which became the objective of not a few currents of philosophical thought.

The Muses

The singing of the celestial choir of the Muses, represented as splendid, graceful young women, delighted their father Zeus and all the other gods. The Muses protected the arts and all that was beautiful; poetry, song, and dance; and inspired human creativity. They also personified various aspects of thought and all, more or less indirectly, recalled the philosophical conceptions that supported the universal value of music. Thus, Calliope is the Muse of epic poetry, Clio of history, Polyhymnia of mime, Euterpe of monody and the flute, Terpsichore of dance and light verse, Erato of choral lyric, Melpomene of tragedy, Thalia of comedy, and Urania of astronomy. In ancient times, therefore, a large part of human creation and knowledge fell under their benevolent protection.

The Graces

The Graces, who were originally conceived of as powerful forces of plant life and only later transformed into exquisite personifications of Beauty, lived with the Muses on Mount Olympus and joined them in their entrancing, sweet songs.
They are traditionally depicted as three charming young women; the figures are almost always depicted nude, immersed in an atmosphere of eternal spring gladdened by enticing sounds, touching hand to shoulder, with the two on the outside looking in one direction and the middle figure turned the other. The Graces exercised a direct and positive influence over work engaging the mind and artistic creation. Later in history, they were worshiped together with Aphrodite.

Zeus coupled with Mnemosyne (Memory) in the pleasant region of Pieria, in Thessaly, for nine consecutive nights. A year later the young Titaness, daughter of Uranus and Gaia, gave birth to nine daughters: **the Muses**.
From his union with the Titaness Eurynome, whose upper body was that of a woman but from the waist down took the form of a fish, Zeus fathered another triad of daughters: **the Charites or Graces**.
In his divine conquests Zeus relied on his manifest powers of persuasion and his considerable seductive charms, resorting to his unchallenged and absolute authority in more difficult cases. His conquests of mortal women, to whose charms he was by no means unsusceptible, often necessitated the use of deception and magical transformations. His union with the Theban woman Semele, daughter of Cadmus and Harmonia, produced the "twice-born" god Dionysus. Semele, like so many of Zeus's illicit loves, was a victim of the jealous Hera, who, mindful of the promise Zeus had made to Semele to grant her anything her mortal heart desired, prompted her to ask Zeus to reveal himself to her in his full splendor. Zeus was thus forced to appear at the height of his power, with lightning and thunderbolts; Semele was reduced to ash, but Zeus had arranged for protecting the yet

Plaster model for Antonio Canova's splendid marble group of the three Graces. Possagno (Italy), Gallery of Plaster Casts, Scarpa Wing.

Disguised as a bull, Zeus captured Europa, the young daughter of king Phoenix, and carried her away across the seas. The myth became widely diffused quite early and was known to the Etruscans, as is evident from this black-figure hydria (ca. 530 BC) probably produced in Cerveteri (ancient Agylla).
Rome, National Museum at Villa Giulia.

Below, Ganymede, the young Trojan prince considered the most beautiful of all mortals, was stolen by Zeus after the Father of the Gods had presented him with a cockerel and a wheel. Detail, red-figure Attic krater, decorated by the Berlin Painter (ca. 500 BC). Paris, Louvre.

Zeus, in the form of a shower of gold, enters the bronze chamber in which the lovely Danae was locked by her father, in a famous painting by Titian (after 1554). Vienna, Kunsthistorisches Museum.

unborn Dionysus by sewing him into his thigh, hidden from Hera's vengeance, until the time came for his delivery. **Leda**, descended from Deucalion, was the wife of Tyndareus, king of Sparta. Zeus became infatuated with her and in order to seduce her transformed himself into a white swan. The egg laid after their union hatched four children: Clytemnestra, later wife of Agamemnon and the mother of Orestes and Electra; Helen, who married Menelaus and whose infidelity occasioned the Trojan wars; and the two Dioscuri ("sons of Zeus"), Castor and Polydeuces. Another of Zeus' celebrated loves was Danae, daughter of Acrisius, king of Argos. The king had received a prophecy to the effect that his daughter Danae would give birth to a son who, upon coming of age, would overthrow and kill his grandfather. In an attempt to escape his destiny, Acrisius imprisoned Danae underground in an inaccessible bronze chamber, where she was nevertheless visited by the amorous Zeus who possessed her as a shower of gold. The fruit of the magical union was Perseus, whose cries revealed his birth to Acrisius. The grandfather placed mother and child in a wooden chest and cast them out to sea; they were washed ashore on the island of Seriphos, where the story of Perseus began to unfold.

Alcmena, the wife of Amphitryon, king of Tiryns, sprang from the noble line of Perseus. Overcome with desire for the beautiful queen, Zeus took advantage of the first absence of the king to appear in his guise and bed her just before his return. That night Alcmena conceived Heracles (fathered by Zeus) and Iphicles (fathered by Amphitryon): the divine origin of the one and the mortal origin of the other were revealed only at their birth.

Europa, instead, the beautiful daughter of king Agenor of Tyre, was playing on the sand with her companions when she was spotted by Zeus. Inflamed with passion, the god transformed himself into a white bull with horns like a crescent moon and lay down at Europa's feet. Although frightened at first, Europa gradually lost her fear and climbed onto the bull's back, whereupon the creature charged toward the sea, ignoring the piteous cries of the maiden clinging to his horns for fear of falling. The bull's headlong flight ended at Crete, where Zeus lay with Europa under an enormous plane tree beside a spring of fresh water. Here were conceived Minos, Sarpedon, and Rhadamanthys. The plane tree, silent witness to the union, was granted the privilege of never losing its leaves.

But Zeus' amorous exuberance did not stop here: the passionate god was also susceptible to the charms of young boys, as we learn from the story of the young Ganymede, a descendent of Dardanus, the first of the royal line of Troy. Ganymede was considered the most beautiful of all mortals, and had just reached adolescence when, while tending his father's herds in the mountains outside Troy, he was approached by the love-smitten Zeus. The god stole him away to Mount Olympus, where he received the gift of eternal youth and became cup-bearer to the Father of the Gods.

Myth in Art

The magical, enthralling (albeit improbable) love story of the noble Leda, queen of Sparta, and the white swan that embodied no less than the Father of the Gods, has beguiled and inspired artists in all historical periods. Many ancient artworks recall the myth; one example is the sculptural group attributed to Timotheus, dated about 360 BC, of which various reproductions were produced in the Roman era. In relatively more recent times, innumerable famous artists, from Leonardo da Vinci to Raphael and from Michelangelo to Correggio, tried their hands at representing the appealing legend, which is also the subject of an extraordinary gem of the jeweler's art: a lapis lazuli plate with an onyx cameo of Leda and the swan, made in Tuscany in the late 1500's and today in the Kunsthistorisches Museum of Vienna.

The Myth of Leda and the Swan

According to another, very early version of this myth, which while little known is not to be dismissed lightly, Zeus would have become infatuated not with Leda but with Nemesis, the goddess of divine vengeance. To escape his embrace she transformed herself into a variety of creatures until, while she was in the form of a goose, Zeus swiftly transformed himself into a swan and had his will of her. This is said to have occurred at Rhamnus, which later became the most important center of worship of the goddess. As the fruit of an undesired love, the egg was abandoned by Nemesis and later found by some shepherds; they gave it to Leda who guarded it safely until the birth of two sets of twins, whom she nurtured as her own children. Identification of Leda with Nemesis, while plausible, is extremely problematic given that the name Leda is not of Greek origin but can be linked etymologically with the ancient Lycian word *lada*, or woman.

A splendid interpretation of the mythical love affair between Leda and the divine swan by Ammannati. Marble group. Florence, Bargello.

Hera, the Mother of the Gods

Hera, the most important of the Olympian goddesses, daughter of Cronos and Rhea and therefore both sister and wife to Zeus, was the protectress of the female world and, as the legitimate wife of the father of all the gods, was also the guardian of wives and of matrimony. As tradition has it, however, the love between Zeus and Hera existed long before their marriage and they were obliged to meet in secret while awaiting the sumptuous official nuptial ceremony.

So often vexed by her husband's many love affairs, Hera became jealous and vindictive not only in dealing with her rivals but also with their progeny, whom she delighted in persecuting: for example, Heracles suffered terribly from her anger, as Hera is attributed with inventing the Twelve Labors. The violent and tragic end suffered by Semele and the goddess' curse on the pregnant Leto are but two other examples of her revengefulness.

Zeus's numerous illicit loves were not the only cause of friction between divine husband and wife, as is evinced by an episode that cost Teiresias his sight. In order to resolve their quarrel over whether the man or the woman drew greater pleasure from the sexual act, they called on Teiresias, whom Zeus had once granted the privilege of experiencing the act from both sides. Teiresias answered that on a scale of one to ten, the man's pleasure could be measured as one while the woman's measured nine, thus supporting Zeus' position. Hera, infuriated at having lost, blinded him, although Zeus rewarded him with the gift of vaticination.

A marvelous head of Hera, portrayed as a young woman with an austere expression, that was once part of a cult statue (ca. 420 BC). Athens, National Archaeological Museum.

Athena, the Strength of Wisdom

The goddess sprang fully grown and fully armed from the head of Zeus and was immediately recognized as almost the alter ego of her father, who presented her with the aegis, the skin of the goat Amalthea. Athena, in truth, is more the goddess of wisdom than of war, which art was the domain of her brother Ares. She did, however, play a decisive role in the Gigantomachy with her many exceptional deeds; for example, she immobilized the Giant Enceladus by hurling against him the whole island of Sicily.
She also intervened strategically in the Trojan wars in direct support of a number of the heroes, among whom Achilles and Odysseus. She guided Perseus with intelligence and stealth to the discovery of those secrets which later enabled him to decapitate the Gorgon, and she constantly protected her favorite hero Heracles throughout his twelve long labors.
According to tradition, Poseidon and Athena put forward rival claims to the possession of Athens and Attica. The contest, in which the prize was bestowal of the victor's name on the city, was judged by the assembled gods who established that the victor would be the one who had offered the most useful gift to the city. Poseidon struck the rock of the Acropolis in Athens with his trident and brought forth a stream of salty water; Athena stamped her foot and there grew up the first olive tree in history. She naturally was victorious, the city took her name, and the olive became a sacred tree—and since then a universal symbol of peace and prosperity.

Athena, with Victory in hand and her the shield hiding the figure of Erichthonius. When Hephaestus attempted to ravish Athena she resisted his advances but was smeared with his seed. She wiped it off with a cloth, which she threw to earth; Gaia thus gave birth to the serpent-son Erichthonius. 2nd century BC copy of the lost statue of Athena Parthenos of Varvakion carved by Phidias between 440 and 430 BC for the Parthenon. Athens, National Archaeological Museum.

Athena with her ever-present owl and Poseidon, holding his trident, before the assembly of the gods. Figured chalice-shaped Etruscan krater (ca. 360 BC). Paris, Louvre.

Athena, goddess of wisdom. Bronze statue (ca. 375 BC) from Piraeus, the port of Athens. Piraeus, Archaeological Museum.

Hephaestus, the Magical Power to Forge Metals

The god of fire and able metalworker Hephaestus was born of Hera, who had conceived him, unfertilized by any male, while she was fuming over Zeus' conception of Athena who he then birthed from his head. Hephaestus was born lame and was cast out by his mother. She threw him down from Olympus; after having slid and rolled for an entire day, he came to rest on the volcanic island of Lemnos, where he set up his forge. To vindicate his cruel rejection by his mother, he fashioned and sent to Hera a magical throne from which the goddess, once seated, was unable to rise. The pleas of the gods to persuade Hephaestus to return to Olympus to free his mother fell on deaf ears until Dionysus made Hephaestus drunk on wine and brought him back straddled over the back of a mule. As a reward to Hephaestus, Zeus gave him the beautiful Aphrodite as his wife—and to Dionysus, for his part in the affair, the honor of officially becoming a member of the Olympian pantheon.

Vulcan's cave in Roman art: a 3rd century AD mosaic from Dougga (Tunisia). Tunis, Musée du Bardo.

Poseidon, Power over the Seas

Considered one of the major Olympian gods (and with Zeus and Hera one of the oldest), Poseidon dominated the seas, which he could agitate as he pleased with a single stroke of his trident; the repercussions could shake the earth and occasion violent earthquakes. He is generally depicted steering his chariot, drawn by dolphins or fabulous sea-creatures, as it swiftly cleaves the waves that rise around but never touch him.

Poseidon fathered almost as many offspring Zeus, but differently from his brother, whose progeny was all benevolent, he begot many creatures of malevolent inclination. His union with the Gorgon Medusa generated the monster Chrysaor, but also the winged horse **Pegasus** (by other traditions, both were born directly from the blood that gushed from the head of Medusa severed by Perseus), while Thoosa bore him the Cyclops Polyphemus—whose later blinding by Odysseus aroused the god's lasting wrath and lengthy persecution of the hero.

Poseidon was a favorite subject among the ancient artists, who systematically imagined him as a powerful, bearded man, often wielding his trident and just as often flanked by a tuna (later substituted by a dolphin). On the coins of Poseidonia (Paestum, Italy) the god was usually shown nude, in the act of throwing his trident. This stance reappears in the famous—and exquisite—bronze statue known as the *Artemision Poseidon* found not far from the coast of the island of Euboea. The god was represented in exactly the same position by Phidias on the west pediment of the Parthenon, while Skopas sculpted him in a celebrated group with Amphitrite and a host of sea dwellers. Lysippus, instead, showed Poseidon nude but at repose, with his foot resting on the prow of a ship. The famous statue by Milo showing an elegantly-draped Poseidon in movement is a superb example of Hellenistic art. It completes the original gallery assembled by the ancients from which the great Roman statuary art drew inspiration and produced its unique interpretations.

Poseidon, the god of the sea, is shown poised to throw his trident (now lost). This bronze statue known as the Artemision Poseidon *was discovered off the island of Euboea. It is attributed to Calamides (ca. 460 BC).* Athens, National Archaeological Museum.

A detail that highlights the extraordinary expressiveness of the face of the Artemision Poseidon*, a masterwork of ancient statuary of exceptionally refined workmanship.*

Pegasus

The winged horse Pegasus was born to the Gorgon Medusa by Poseidon, or, according to the legend traceable to Hesiod, sprang forth with his brother Chrysaor from the neck of his pregnant mother when Perseus decapitated her. He flew immediately to Olympus, where he entered Zeus' service; later, while he was drinking at the fountain Peirene, he was captured by Bellerophon (to whom, by another tradition, he was instead given by Poseidon). After having bridled him, Bellerophon rode him when he defeated the Chimaera and in the battle against the Amazons. At his rider's death, Pegasus returned to Olympus to pull Zeus' thunder chariot. With a stamp of his hoof (by order of Poseidon), Pegasus arrested the rise of Mount Helicon—which was being pushed skyward by its pleasure in hearing the songs of the Pierides, in competition with the Muses—and thus produced the Hippocrene ("The Horse's Spring"). Later yet, Pegasus was transformed into a constellation of stars.

A deceased couple is carried into the Underworld by the winged horse Pegasus. Greek terracotta relief (ca. 450 BC) from Locri (Italy). Taranto (Italy), National Archaeological Museum.

Demeter, the Fertility of the Earth

In contrast to Gaia, Mother Earth, the Earth understood as a cosmogonic element and thus genetrix of all things, Demeter is the goddess of cultivated land and thus of fruit and, above all, of grain, a product which plays a fundamental role in her story and especially in that of her daughter by Zeus, Persephone. Persephone's carefree childhood in the company of her sisters Athena and Artemis, also daughters of Zeus, ended when her uncle Hades, Zeus' brother and lord of the Underworld, became enraptured with her. Demeter was unwilling to marry her daughter to Hades and condemn her to eternal reclusion in the realm of shadows: Hades thus snatched the girl away while she was picking flowers near the entrance to the Underworld at Eleusis (or, in another version, near the foot of Mount Aetna in Sicily).

Desperate over the sudden and mysterious disappearance of her daughter, Demeter wandered all the known world in search of Persephone for nine days and nine nights; she neither ate nor drank, nor did she wash or attend to her appearance in any way—she simply followed the light of the two flaming torches she carried. At one point in her travels, in the guise of old woman, Demeter came to Eleusis where she sat down to rest on a stone later called *aghélastos petra* ("stone without joy") in memory of her suffering. Demeter then visited the court of king Celeus of Eleusis, where she found refuge and refreshment and even one of her old servants, Iambe, who coaxed smiles from the goddess with her playful stories. In recognition of the kind welcome she had received, Demeter revealed the secrets of the cultivation of grain to Triptolemus, the youngest of Celeus's sons, and sent him about the world teaching agriculture. Not surprisingly, the most important of all the ancient sanctuaries to Demeter and Persephone grew up at Eleusis around the sacred stone where the saddened goddess had rested. Her cult was founded on the mysteries of fertility, revealed only to the initiated.

As a result of Demeter's voluntary exile from Olympus the earth became barren and the natural order of the world, reflected in the normal cycle of the seasons, fell into in total confusion. Zeus was forced to intervene: he ordered his brother Hades to free Persephone and return her to her mother. But this was no longer possible: Persephone had eaten a seed from a pomegranate despite having been warned that in order to return to the earth she must abstain from any sustenance in the Underworld. But Zeus found an acceptable compromise: he arranged that Persephone should spend a part of the year in the Underworld and the other with her mother Demeter, who could in this manner return to Mount Olympus and re-establish the natural order. Thus the Greeks explained the seasons: each spring, Persephone fled the Underworld, emerging from her subterranean abode as the first seedlings germinated in the fields. During the whole time her daughter was underground, the cold winter season, Demeter made the earth barren and unproductive.

Persephone, holding a candle, benevolently observes and offers her blessing as Demeter, holding her scepter, hands the sheaves of grain to Triptolemus, the youngest son of the king of Eleusis. Triptolemus passed on the gift to men at large. Relief (ca. 430-420 BC) from Eleusis, where the famed Eleusinian Mysteries were celebrated yearly. Athens, National Archaeological Museum.

Praxiteles

The celebrated 4th century BC Athenian sculptor, master of marble and all its secrets, was undoubtedly one of the most highly-quoted artists of the ancient world, the author of outstanding and more than once imitated masterpieces. Among Praxiteles' works, all distinguished by harmonious plasticism and gentle, sinuous rhythms, perhaps the most important was the universally famous *Aphrodite of Cnidus*, which brought fame to the island that hosted this nude portrayal of the goddess. The statue, of which many copies were made, was destroyed in the fire that razed Constantinople—whence it had been transferred. Other masterpieces are *Artemis* portrayed in the act of drawing an arrow from her quiver; *Apollo Sauroctonus* ("killing a lizard" with an arrow), the original of which was probably in bronze but which we know through more than seventy marble copies; *Triptolemus* enthroned; and above all the *Hermes* now preserved in the Museum of Olympia. This statue comes from the Temple of Hera and is believed by the majority of critics to be the original, although some attribute it to a Praxiteles who lived in the 2nd century BC. The god is shown in the nude at the height of his young beauty (in accordance with the artist's accepted aesthetic canons, which called for humanizing the gods' aspect), holding in his left hand the tiny Dionysus while with his raised right he attempts to distract the boy by pointing out a bunch of grapes.

Hermes, the Messenger of the Gods

Although Hermes is known mostly as the messenger of the Olympian gods, he was also the god of shepherds; in fact, he is frequently depicted as Criophorus—that is, Hermes the ram-bearer. He is also the god of cunning and of shrewdness, and of barter and therefore of commerce as well as of theft.

Hermes was born to the Nymph Maia in a cave on Mount Cyllene in Arcadia; he had been fathered by Zeus in the dead of night while all the other gods and mortals slept. He was born on the fourth day of the month, which ever since has been consecrated to him (in the Roman world he was called Mercury, and hence the French and Italian names for Wednesday: *mercredi* and *mercoledì*).

Shortly after his birth, still in swaddling bands in his cradle, he showed amazing precocity: he wriggled free and ran to far-off Thessaly, where his half-brother Apollo was grazing his cattle. Hermes stole several of the herd and, after having secured a leafy branch to the tail of each animal to obliterate their tracks, led them back to Greece where he hid them in a grotto near the city of Pylos. He then re-

Hermes with the young Dionysus in his arms. Marble statue discovered in the Temple of Hera at Olympia, probably an original work by the great Athenian sculptor ***Praxiteles*** *(ca. 340 BC).* Olympia, Archaeological Museum.

turned to his mother's cave on Mount Cyllene, but before wrapping himself again in his swaddling bands he killed a tortoise, hollowed out its shell and strung it with cords made of the intestines of some of the cattle stolen from Apollo, thus fashioning the first lyre. Apollo, when he realized he had been robbed, remonstrated with Maia, who, seeing Hermes swaddled innocently in the cradle as she had left him, refused to believe the god's accusations.

It was thus that Zeus intervened to demand that the cattle be returned, but Apollo, enchanted by the sound of the newly invented lyre, accepted it in exchange for his animals and became a master of the instrument. It is also recounted that later on, as he was tending the cattle he had had from Apollo, Hermes invented the multiple-flute reed pipe, or syrinx. This time, Apollo offered in exchange his golden staff, or caduceus, which became the symbol of Hermes in his role as messenger of the gods, and therefore of all ambassadors.

One of Hermes' tasks as messenger of the gods was to accompany the spirits of the dead to the Underworld, the entrance to which was guarded by two fierce sphinxes that prevented any contact between the world of the living and that of the dead. Attic black-figure oinochoe (ca. 560 BC). Athens, National Archaeological Museum.

Hermes fighting Ares and Poseidon on a red-figure vase. Athens, National Archaeological Museum.

Aphrodite, Beauty and Love

The daughter of Zeus and Dione (or alternatively, born from the testicles of Uranus when they were severed and thrown into the sea by Cronos), Aphrodite was the goddess of love and of beauty. She was married to Hephaestus, the lame god of fire, but her great love was Ares and their oft-sung amorous adventures provoked Hephaestus' wrath and vengeance. On one occasion he literally "caught" Aphrodite and Ares together in Aphrodite's bed in a magical fishing net—and then summoned all the gods to laugh at the lovers' predicament. From the union of Aphrodite and Ares sprang Eros and Anteros (literally, "love" and "return-love"), Deimos and Phobos ("rout" and "panic"), Harmonia, the future wife of Cadmus, king of Thebes, and lastly Priapus, the god of gardens. Among her earthly loves was the noble Trojan hero Anchises, who fathered Aeneas, progenitor of the founder of Rome; it was Aeneas' immortal origin that fed the flourishing Roman worship of his mother as Venus. Aphrodite's role in the Trojan War was anything but secondary and went far beyond her love for Anchises. In a certain sense, her beauty was even the cause of the war—the story runs thus. At the wedding of Peleus and Thetis, the future parents of the great Achilles, Eris ("discord") tossed out an apple for she who would be judged most beautiful: Hera, Athena, or Aphrodite. Zeus suggested that Paris, prince of Troy, decide the contest. The three goddesses came before Paris at Troas, each proclaiming her superior beauty and promising him the most wonderful of gifts: Hera promised him sovereignty over all Asia and Athena invincibility in war, but neither of these gifts rivaled the hand of Helen, the most beautiful of mortal woman, promised to him by Aphrodite. And so Aphrodite won the contest—and Helen's abduction was instrumental in causing the most celebrated of wars.

During the hostilities, Aphrodite unceasingly supported Troy, and although she was unable to avoid defeat, her protection of Anchises, their son Aeneas, and his son Ascanius (also known as Iulus) prevented the extermination of the royal Trojan line.

The goddess Aphrodite modestly covers her beauty as she steps from the water. Marble Roman copy of a Greek original (1st cent. BC). Athens, National Archaeological Museum.

A detail of the Aphrodite found in the House of Menander in Pompeii. Naples, National Archaeological Museum.

The goddess of beauty is born from a shell and emerges from the white foam of the waves. Terracotta votive statue (4th cent. BC). Athens, National Archaeological Museum.

The pure beauty of Aphrodite is born from the waters on a half shell, while one of the Horai (according to the Ovidian tradition, which was perfectly assimilated by Humanistic literature) offers the goddess a splendid cloak. To her right, Chloris and Zephyrus, whose breath ripples the sea and blows Aphrodite toward shore, which may be Sicily. Tempera on canvas, The Birth of Venus *by Alessandro Botticelli (1484-86).* Florence, Uffizi.

Ares, the Frenzy of War

Ares, the son of Hera and Zeus, was the god of war and all things martial. He was involved not only in heroic events on the mythological scale but also in "low" enterprises linked to war and is in fact represented in the literary sources as enjoying carnage and bloodshed. In the Trojan War, he intervened at times alongside the Trojans, at times allied with the Greeks, almost at random, according to which side was momentarily best suited for satisfying his caprices. Many of his adventures took place in Thrace, a wild area in the north of Greece inhabited by his daughters, the Amazons, born of his union with the Nymph Harmonia. Although he frequently took a leading role in conflicts, Ares was rarely victorious; more often than not, he retreated in disgrace, as when he deserted Hector in his conflict with Diomedes or when he withdrew from the ranks of the gods under the walls of Troy. On both these occasions he took refuge on Mount Olympus because Athena—directly or indirectly—had made his position untenable. At other times his brute fury was matched, to his detriment, against the calculated cunning of Heracles, as in the fatal encounter between the hero and Ares's son Cycnus.

The story of the affair between Ares and Aphrodite, who was the legitimate spouse of Hephaestus, was popular in ancient times. Attic relief (5th cent. BC). Venice, Archaeological Museum.

A bronze Greek statuette of the young Apollo, showing the god in all his elegant splendor (1st cent. BC). Vienna, Kunsthistorisches Museum.

Apollo, Light and Purity

A radiant god shedding benevolent light, the Sun arisen from the womb of night (Apollo's mother Leto's name in fact signifies "the hidden one"), Apollo symbolized the triumph of day over the dark powers of the shadows, and therefore all the beneficent powers and positive effects of the light and warmth of sunshine. He was venerated as Targelion, the fertile warmth that ripens fruit (the name Targelion has also come to indicate the month of May); as Smintheus (from *sminthos*, mouse) and as Parnopius (from *parnops*, grasshopper), he was worshiped as the destroyer of rats and locusts and as man's liberator from the plagues these creatures brought. He was also the divine inspirer of every lyrical beauty, and therefore of music and poetry, and he directed the choir of the Muses, daughters of Zeus and Mnemosyne. His symbols are thus the bow and arrows, clearly references to the sun god who could wound with the dart of his rays, the laurel that encircled his brow, and the cithara that he played with a plectrum.

The swan, the wolf, and the dolphin were sacred to him: the swan, because at the moment of his birth on the seventh day of the month a flock of swans made seven circuits of the island of Delos where he was born; the wolf, because Apollo puts to flight this beast that causes such terror in the winter (Apollo was also worshiped as Lyceius, from *lykos*, wolf); and the dolphin, because Apollo often assumed its form to cross the waves swiftly, and not infrequently to save the shipwrecked.

The most famous of his attributes is, however, the tripod, which clearly alludes to the **divinatory powers** and the gift of prophecy he governed and which he could grant to the priestesses of his sanctuaries. Apollo had visited Delphi, in Phocis, and killed with his arrows the dragon Python that protected an **oracle** of the goddess of law,

Apollo, the beautiful god of music, shown crowned with laurel on an Attic plate. Delphi, Archaeological Museum.

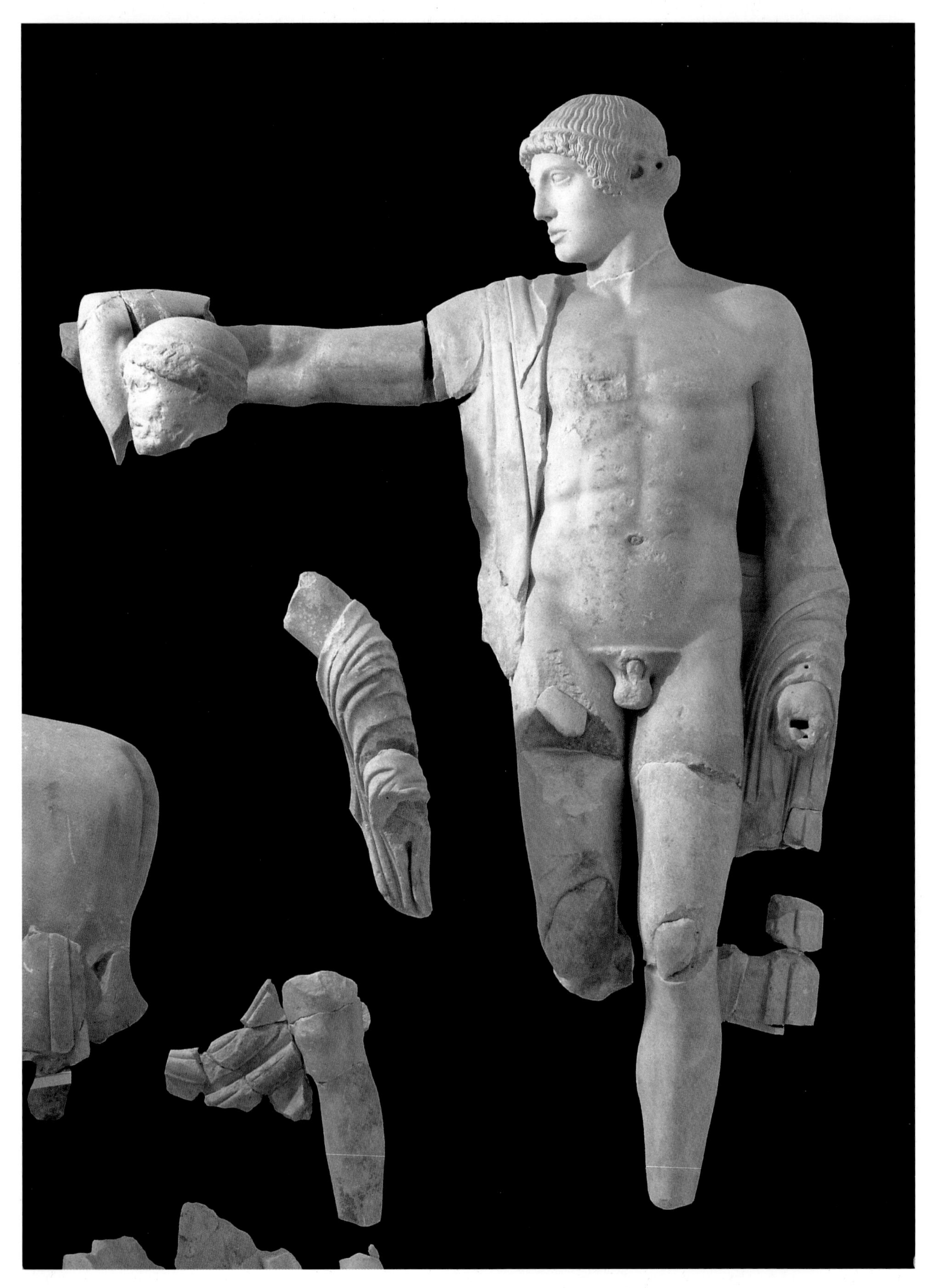

Apollo, the God of Oracles and Divination

The oracles, a typical institution of the Greek world, arose in places sacred to gods and were generally entrusted to the care of a group of priests who acted as interpreters for the god, to whom they submitted queries only after having successfully performed certain preliminary rites of purification and sacrifice. Besides the inevitable Zeus, another typically oracular divinity was Apollo, with famous sanctuaries at Delphi, Didyma, and Claros, and others in Troas, Lycia, and Boeotia. Delphi, in particular, early on assumed political importance, since the oracle served not only common citizens but also Greek and foreign governments, which posed queries relating to important questions of domestic and foreign policy; for example, generally no one set out to found new colony before having consulted an oracle. Thus, many of the most important cities often did everything in their power to influence the responses of the oracles and above all those of Apollo, which were very much respected in the ancient world. The responses given by the oracles generally referred to questions submitted in written form by the priest, who then undertook to interpret and expound the vaticination of the god as pronounced by a man or woman (like the famous Pythia) in an induced ecstatic state.

This page, the oracle of Apollo at Delphi. Fragment of a Greek vase (4th cent. BC). Taranto (Italy), National Archaeological Museum.

Left, Apollo raising his arm to declare the victory of the Lapiths over the Centaurs. Detail of the west pediment from the Temple of Zeus at Olympia (ca. 460 BC). Olympia, Archaeological Museum.

Themis. The oracle was a chasm in the earth that emitted fumes capable of inducing trance and the power to pronounce prophecies. The dragon, instead of staying at his post, roamed the countryside and wreaked every sort of devastation in the region, destroying crops, killing farmers, sacking villages, and even polluting springs and streams. After having slaughtered Python and taken possession of the oracle, Apollo took on the epithet Pythios; he bestowed a bronze tripod on the sanctuary and granted divinatory powers to one of the priestesses, who was known as the Pythia ever after. Seated on Apollo's great tripod, the priestess inhaled the vapors from the chasm and chewed laurel leaves; to the questions asked her she gave "sibylline" responses, which were then unraveled by a host of sacred interpreters whose only task was to render intelligible the meaning of the prophecies.

As the god of beauty, and therefore also of physical perfection and high morals, Apollo was represented as the most attractive of the gods, tall and with a fine head of hair; it is no wonder that he had many amorous adventures, with mortals and goddesses alike. The young god of love Eros, irritated by Apollo's teasing and annoyed by his mockery of his first

clumsy attempts with the bow and arrow (with which the older god was extremely skillful), one day decided to have his revenge: he provoked Apollo's infatuation with Daphne, the beautiful daughter of the Thessalian river god Peneus. Daphne, however, had no intention of submitting to the god's embrace and fled into the mountains. Apollo pursued her and a moment before he overcame her Peneus, in answer to his daughter's prayers, transformed her into a laurel tree (*daphne* in Greek), which from that time on was sacred to Apollo. Apollo also dallied with the Nymphs; one of their number, Cyrene, bore him Aristaeus, the demigod who taught men dairy skills, bee-keeping, vine cultivation and wine-making, and the use of nets and traps in hunting. His most well-known mortal love was Hecuba, the wife of Priam, king of Troy, who gave birth to Troilus, the youngest prince of the royal line. An oracle had predicted that if Troilus lived to be twenty Troy could not be conquered; thus, during the Trojan war, Achilles ambushed Troilus when he crept secretly from the city with his sister Polyxena to visit a spring: he to water the horses, she to draw water in a vase. Apollo also loved Troilus' sister, Cassandra, the daughter of Hecuba and Priam, and seduced her with a promise to reveal to her the art of prophecy. But after having received her instruction Cassandra refused his love, and Apollo condemned her to the fate of always prophesying truly but never being believed. Finally, from Apollo's union with Coronis, daughter of the king of the Lapiths, was born the god of medicine Asclepias.
Apollo did not disdain love with members of his own sex, notably **Hyacinthus** and **Cyparissus**, whose deaths—or better, their metamorphoses into a flower and a tree—stand as reminders of the god's close association with the forces of nature.

Apollo in combat with Heracles for possession of the sacred (and prophetic) tripod that stood in his sanctuary at Delphi. Red-figure amphora (ca. 510 BC) decorated by the Athenian painter Phintias. Tarquinia, National Archaeological Museum.

Apollo flying on a swan, one of his sacred animals, to the land of the Hyperboreans. Fragment, from the Acropolis of Athens, of a red-figure plate decorated by the great Athenian painter Euphronius (ca. 510 BC) and dedicated as a votive offering. Athens, National Archaeological Museum.

Hyacinthus

Hyacinthus, son of Amyclas and Diomedes, was a young Spartan prince whose extraordinary beauty inflamed the passions of Apollo. While the two were throwing the discus together one day, Zephyr, the god of the west wind, jealous of Apollo because he too was attracted by Hyacinth, blew the discus off course. It dashed against Hyacinthus' temple and struck him dead. The grief-stricken Apollo, to immortalize the memory of his companion, made a flower grow from the drops of his blood where they had fallen to earth: the hyacinth, with its red markings. In Alexander's time, this myth, which weaves through ancient art, became the symbol of the fragility of young plants, which wither rapidly if exposed to the rays of a too-ardent sun.

Cyparissus

Cyparissus, a handsome young man of Ceos, son of Telephus and a descendent of Heracles, was loved and pampered by Apollo, who gave him one of his sacred deer as a token of his love. The tame animal became the boy's faithful companion, but one summer's day while the deer lay sleeping in the shade of some bushes Cyparissus slew it by mistake with his javelin. In desperation, he wanted only to die, but first implored Apollo that his tears might fall for all eternity. The god transformed him into a tree, the cypress, the symbol of sorrow with its "tears" (either the cypress's small globular cones or the trickles of sap that streak its trunk) always in evidence.

Artemis, the Virgin Huntress

Artemis, Apollo's twin sister and daughter of Leto, was born on the island of Delos just before her brother but nevertheless ready to assist their mother at his birth. She chose the eternal youth offered to virgins and dedicated herself exclusively to the adventurous life of the hunt, armed with her bow and arrows. The goddess was also held responsible for sudden and painless deaths and for deaths of women in childbirth.

The arrogant and vindictive Artemis was relentless in her persecution of those who offended her. Against Oeneus, for example, who had failed to perform a sacrifice in her honor, she sent the monstrous wild boar of Calydon. The Giant hunter son of Poseidon, Orion, who had attempted to take her by violence, was stung on the heel by one of her scorpions and killed: both scorpion and victim were transformed into constellations, with Orion always appearing to take flight from Scorpio.

She transformed Aritaeus' son Actaeon, who had chanced to spy her while she bathed nude in a spring, into a stag and set Actaeon's own pack of fifty hounds on him; the dogs, not recognizing their master in his new guise, tore him to pieces and then searched vainly throughout the forest, baying for their lost master, until the Centaur Chiron took pity on them and modeled a statue in the image of Actaeon.

A similar fate awaited Callisto, virgin huntress and companion of the goddess in the chase. She was seduced by Zeus, who had disguised himself as Artemis (as Callisto would let no man near her); her pregnancy was revealed when she undressed to bathe at a spring; in due time, she became mother of Arcas, the eponymous hero of Arcadia. Artemis, out of vengeance for Callisto's infidelity, exiled her and transformed her into a bear, whom she hunted and killed with her arrows; but Zeus took pity on his lover and turned her into the constellation of the Great Bear.

Artemis, the captivating goddess of the hunt. Greek bronze statue of the Classical era (mid-4th cent. BC). Piraeus, Archaeological Museum.

Dionysus, the Inebriating Power of Wine

One of the most important of the second generation of gods, Dionysus, known to the Romans as Bacchus, was the god of wine and of viticulture; more generally, he personified the energy of Nature that ripens fruit thanks to the beneficial effects of water. The god is associated with the humid element indispensable to vegetation throughout his story: tradition relates how Dionysus ("born twice") was birthed from Zeus, who had sewn him into his thigh after his mortal mother Semele was reduced to ash when she beheld her divine lover in his full splendor. The infant Dionysus was carried by Hermes to the Nymphs of Mount Nysa, who saw to his up bringing. The "naturalistic" meaning of the myth is obvious: Semele was the earth scorched by the violent rays of the summer sun, but the fruit of her womb, Dionysus, the life-giving warmth that brings things to maturation, was saved and sustained by the Water Nymphs, the clouds that irrigate the earth. Raised in the lush, wild woods, Dionysus later planted vines and became drunk on the sweet juice of its fruits. Crowned with vine-leaves and ivy, he traveled the world on a magical chariot drawn by panthers and habitually followed by a band of boisterous companions: the satyrs, men with horse's tails, goat's hooves, and large animal ears, and the **Maenads**, women who danced in trance, overcome with the ecstasy provoked by the god. In his travels, Dionysus taught men the arts of cultivating the land and of viticulture, he founded new cities, and he instituted cults in his name wherever he stopped. He was a divine spokesman of new values and a new, more joyous and sociable approach to life.

With a small satyr curled at his feet and a cup of wine raised aloft, Sansovino's portrayal of Dionysus is known for its sober, unusually placid elegance and its plasticity. Florence, Bargello.

Dionysus, the god of wine. Head of a marble statue (3rd cent. BC) from the sanctuary of the god on the island of Thasos. Thasos, Archaeological Museum.

The Bacchantes

The unruly, boisterous, jubilant band that accompanied the God of Wine wherever he went included the satyrs and the god Pan but also the Bacchantes or Maenads (or Thyiads), female participants in the typical orgiastic worship of Dionysus. In their abandon to the powerful attraction exerted by the god, induced or helped along by the inebriating effects of Dionysus' wine, they attained a state of ecstasy such that with their bare hands they could tear apart the young animals destined for sacrifice. The first Bacchantes, it is said, were the Nymphs who raised the young god; later, they were joined by true priestesses and female initiates who celebrated Dionysus' mysteries with dances and orgies. In ancient art, the Bacchantes were usually represented in a state of frenetic excitement, dressed in light, translucent shifts (when they were not partially nude and covered only with goat or panther pelts) uniquely belted with ivy tendrils or lengths of grapevine. They often carried lighted torches or held the thyrsus, the sacred wand wreathed in ivy and topped by a pine cone, and danced to the sound of the tympans, cymbals, and double pipes, totally enraptured by the repetitive rhythmical beat of the music typical of the festive band that kept company with the God of Wine.

A priestess of Dionysus in all her hieratic aloofness. Detail of a painted Greek amphora (4th cent. BC). Paestum (Italy), National Museum.

A Maenad in Dionysian ecstasy, holding the thyrsus (the sacred branch crowned with a pinecone and covered with ivy) in one hand and a situla (a small bucket) of wine in the other. She moves to the rhythmical and repetitive music of the double flute, the typical accompaniment to Dionysian revels. Detail of a drawing on a red-figure krater of Siculan (early Sicilian) production (ca. 340 BC). Lipari (Italy), Archaeological Museum.

Knavish and rubicund, crowned by vine leaves and grapes, stretched out like a later young Roman on his triclinium. Thus Dionysus, god of wine and the ecstasy it induces, was depicted by the extraordinary brush of Caravaggio in the late 16th century.
Florence, Uffizi.

On one of Dionysus' many travels, a voyage to the island of Naxos, his ship was approached by a Tyrrhenian pirate vessel. The god was disguised as a curly-haired boy wearing a purple cloak, and the pirates, unaware of his true identity, captured him and then headed east with the intention of selling him as a slave. In an instant, Dionysus revealed all his divine power: he immobilized the ship with garlands while grapevines bourgeoned all over, he transformed the oars into serpents, and, while the planks sprouted ivy tendrils, made lions and panthers appear from nowhere. The terrified pirates abandoned ship, but as they dived into the sea they were transformed by the god into dolphins. On Naxos, Dionysus saved Ariadne, who had been abandoned there by Theseus, and took her to Olympus—not before completing his mission of educating men in the art of cultivation and establishing his cult throughout the world.
Worshiped as a great benefactor of mankind and for this reason associated with other benevolent

Dionysus in the vineyards. Detail of a Greek amphora decorated by the Priam Painter (520-510 BC). Rome, National Museum at Villa Giulia.

Sileni at the wine-press. Detail of a Greek krater decorated by the Leningrad Painter (5th cent. BC). Lecce (Italy), Provincial Museum.

deities like Apollo and Demeter, Dionysus was regarded as the god who, through the effects of his "magical" drink, most lifted man's spirits, encouraged song, and inspired poetry while alleviating the cares and sufferings of the body and the mind. But while moderate worship of Dionysus (or rather, the moderate use of his wine) could offer man a better quality of life, the god was also capable of deranging the human mind with his potent ecstasies, as we see in the stories of Lycurgus and Pentheus.

Lycurgus, king of Thrace and an adversary of the cult of Dionysus, refused to receive the youthful god when he passed through his lands with his loud and unruly band of followers. He even tried to arrest Dionysus, but unsuccessfully, since the god took refuge at sea with the Nereid Thetis (the mother of the great Achilles); Lycurgus had to be content with imprisoning the Bacchantes. The god took his revenge by miraculously freeing the Bacchantes of their fetters and driving Lycurgus mad: the king immediately fell prey to severe hallucinations; he took an axe and severed his young son's legs and one of his own, all in the belief that he was cutting down grapevines. When he recovered his sanity, he realized that by opposing Dionysus he had brought about not only his downfall and his son's but also afflictions on his people, since the god sent a severe drought on the whole land.

The oracles revealed that the blame lay solely with Lycurgus' arrogance; the king was thus put to death by his own people, who tied him arms and legs to four wild horses so that he was torn apart as they spooked the animals to run in different directions.

Pentheus, king of Thebes, tried to prevent the Theban women from celebrating the Dionysian rites, despite repeated warnings to the contrary from the soothsayer Teiresias. Pentheus tried to chain Dionysus and scorned his power even though the god performed many prodigious acts like dissolving

The drunken Dionysus crowned with the leaves and fruit of the grapevine, a plant sacred to him, and accompanied by a small satyr. Marble Roman statue, copy of a Hellenistic original (2nd century BC). Athens, National Archaeological Museum.

the chains intended to fetter him and destroying the royal palace with flames. Pentheus then went to Mount Cithaeron and concealed himself in a hollow tree to observe the Theban women in their Dionysian revels, the sight of which was prohibited to the uninitiated. But the ceremony was well advanced and the women, inflamed with Dionysian ecstacy, spied their king and in their frenzy took him for an animal which they tore limb from limb with their bare hands and sacrificed to Dionysus. His own mother, Agave, tore off his head, and believing it to be that of a lion impaled it on a branch and carried it in triumph to Thebes. After the ceremony, Agave and the other women realized what had occurred and understood how great was the power of Dionysus, who had chosen to punish an act of sacrilege in such a terrible manner. Filled with remorse, Agave fled Thebes.

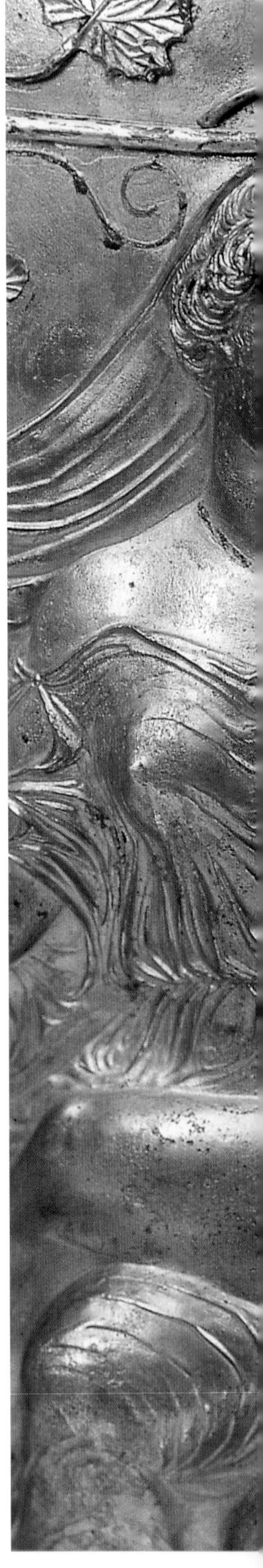

Dionysus and Ariadne. The god is shown nude in a sensual pose expressive of the voluptuous abandon induced by drinking wine, with his leg draped gently over the thigh of his lover Ariadne. Dionysus' infatuation with the princess saved her after she was abandoned by Theseus on the island of Naxos. Detail of a krater with two handles in gilt bronze (ca. 340 BC), from a tomb discovered at Derveni in Macedonia. Thessalonika, Archaeological Museum.

Titian's dramatic interpretation of the moment in which Dionysus, followed by his procession of satyrs and Bacchantes, meets Ariadne alone and despairing on the island of Naxos where she was abandoned by Theseus. The god fell in love with the unfortunate maiden at first sight, and as a token of his love transformed her crown into a constellation. London, National Gallery.

Hestia, the Safety of the Domestic Hearth

Hestia was the sister of Zeus and Hera and the goddess of the domestic hearth; at the same time, she was its personification as the center of all family life. Thus, while all the other gods and goddesses left Mount Olympus at one time or another, Hestia never did: as the hearth was the religious center of the house, so was Hestia the religious heart of the celestial dwelling-place. Since fire was instrumental in family religious sacrifices, the images of the household divinities always appeared beside the hearth; thus, in a certain sense, Hestia also represented the temple of domestic religion and played a fundamental role in all the ceremonies celebrated in the family circle. And as every house was therefore also her temple, there were no sacred buildings dedicated to the goddess—but she was worshiped throughout in Greece in every temple, whatsoever its dedication; all sacrificial ceremonies began and ended with a libation to Hestia; she also claimed her part of every ceremonial feast, and enjoyed the privilege of being mentioned first in prayers; and in all ceremonies and sacrifices she was always offered the freshest fruits of the earth. As fire is the symbol of purity, so the goddess was conceived chaste and pure—and so she chose to remain: repeated offers of marriage from both Apollo and Poseidon met with firm refusals, as nothing could shake her resolve to remain eternally virgin. And virgin too (or at least, extremely chaste) were her priestesses and the women who participated in her ceremonies. The hearth of Hestia in the temple of Apollo at Delphi, with its ever-burning fire, became a symbol of unity acknowledged by all the peoples of Greece.

Hestia holding a bouquet of flowers. Greek art, detail of a large figured bowl. Tarquinia (Italy), National Archaeological Museum.

Asclepias, Salvation in Medicine

Many different traditions relate the birth of Asclepias, the god of medicine: some refer to him as the son of Apollo and Coronis ("the crow" in Greek), daughter of Phlegyas, the Thessalian king of the Lapiths, while others say he was born of Apollo and Arsinoe, the daughter of Leucippus, king of Messenia—but the first-mentioned story is the most widely accepted. By it, Apollo fell in love with Coronis, and Asclepias was conceived by their union; during her pregnancy, however, Coronis betrayed Apollo with a mortal. The god, informed of the misdeed by a crow (or, by other accounts, by his own power of divination), took his vengeance by killing Coronis. As she lay on her funeral pyre, Apollo rescued his unborn child by extracting him from his mother's breast, and entrusted the good Centaur Chiron with his upbringing. Chiron taught the child the art of medicine, in which Asclepias soon excelled and even discovered how to resuscitate the dead with the blood of the Gorgon, which he had received from Athena. This practice sparked the envy of Zeus, who, fearing that the numerous resurrections enacted by Asclepias would overthrow the existing cosmic order, hurled a thunderbolt and slew him. Apollo then avenged his son's death by killing the Cyclops' who fashioned Zeus' thunderbolts and by withdrawing from Olympus for a time. After his death, Asclepias appeared as a constellation, Serpens (from the snakes that coiled around his staff, the symbol of his healing power). Asclepias was therefore a benevolent god, capable of bestowing physical well-being and curing illness. He was venerated in many parts of Greece, and in particular at Epidaurus in Argolis as well as at Sicyon, Athens, Pergamus, and Smyrna, and later in Rome on the Isola Tiberina. Every sanctuary had a hospital where pilgrim/patients gathered to be treated with poultices and tisanes as well as by surgery—but mainly by recitation of magic formulae and the incubation method: prayers and sacrifices induced sleep so that Asclepias could appear in dreams and suggest remedies.

Above, a Classical-era head of Hygiea, goddess of health, daughter of Asclepias and Epione. The beneficent goddess is often represented accompanied by her father, from whom she inherited the attribute of the entwined serpent. Athens, National Archaeological Museum.

Right, Asclepias, the god of medicine, leaning on a stick entwined with a serpent, the symbol of his medicinal powers, as he and his children receive a family of supplicants whom he will bless with his cures. Marble votive relief (ca. 360 BC) from the sanctuary of Asclepias.
Athens, National Archaeological Museum.

Hades, the Shadowy Realm of the Underworld

Hades was born of the union of Cronos and Rhea was thus the brother of Zeus, Poseidon, and Hera. After the victory over the Titans, Zeus divided rule of the cosmos with the other male offspring of Cronos; to Hades fell dominion over the Underworld, the kingdom of the dead. His control over dead souls was absolute and his will implacable; he permitted no one to return to the land of the living. In his exercise of power he was served by various demons and genii who carried out his

Hades, god of the Underworld, and Persephone. Cerberus, guardian of the gates, sits at the feet of Hades. Marble Roman statue from the sanctuary of the goddess Isis at Gortyn, Crete (2nd century AD). Herakleion, Archaeological Museum.

Hades and Persephone enthroned in the kingdom of the Underworld. Terracotta votive relief (ca. 470 BC) from the sanctuary of the goddess at Locri Epizephyrii (now Locri, Calabria, Italy). Reggio Calabria (Italy), National Archaeological Museum.

orders (Charon, the Styx ferryman, is one of the most well known and is mentioned in Dante's *Inferno*). But this largely malevolent god had a positive side to his nature, as is evinced by his epithet Pluton or Pluto ("the rich one"): as lord of the Underworld he contributed to the fertility of the earth's surface land and also supervised her internal riches; that is, her wealth of minerals.

Hades rarely visited the earth and is seldom involved in the myths, although he does play a fundamental role in the story of Demeter and Persephone.

Pan, the Joys of Rural Life

Pan, according to some traditions the son of Cronos and Rhea, and to others the son of Hermes and a Nymph, was the god of shepherds and their flocks. He was originally worshiped in Arcadia but later in the whole of Greece—and beyond. Pan is usually represented as half man and half animal, his lower parts being those of a goat and his upper part in the nature of a man, but with two horns sprouting from his head. It is told that his horrifying appearance caused his mother to abandon him at birth. The infant Pan was found by Hermes, who took him up to Olympus. He was welcomed with benevolence by all the gods, but especially by Dionysus who included him in his band of satyrs and sileni (with whom Pan had strong affinities in both appearance and behavior). He is often shown holding a multiple-flute reed pipe, the panpipe or syrinx, which not surprisingly became a favorite instrument among shepherds; he was extremely agile and a fast runner, and could climb rocks as nimbly as any goat. He haunted the shady woods, often near cool streams or secluded shrubbery, where he spied the doings of Nymphs and ephebes (whom he loved equally) or slept away the hottest hours of the day, much as the shepherds do. His frenzied lust for physical contact with Nymphs and youths represents the vital force of nature, especially its carnal and sexual aspects.

Pan admiring Aphrodite, who shakes a scolding sandal at him. Marble sculptural group (ca. 100 BC) from Delos. Athens, National Archaeological Museum.

CHAPTER III

THE HEROES: THE IMMORTAL VIRTUES

HERACLES: THE SIGNS OF FUTURE GREATNESS

One of Zeus' many loves was the mortal Alcmena, wife of the Amphitryon, king of Tiryns. Following the death of Alcmena's brothers in a feud and an unfortunate accident in which Alcmena's father Electryon (grandson of Perseus, and king of Mycenae before abdicating in favor of Amphitryon) was killed, Amphitryon and Alcmena were forced to take refuge at the court of Creon at Thebes. While Amphitryon was away from Thebes at war against the Teleboae (early inhabitants of the island of Leucadia), Zeus fell in love with Alcmena and contrived to appear to her in her husband's guise to Alcmena and conceive the most celebrated of the Greek heroes, Heracles, who as Zeus' son was also a demigod. When Amphitryon returned he discovered how Zeus had deceived his wife and had his way with her; only the direct intercession of Zeus himself convinced Amphitryon to forgive his innocent wife. Thus the two made up—and made love—and since their union was fertile they conceived another child. Alcmena thus bore twins, Heracles and his brother Iphicles, who was the "younger" by only one night, as Amphitryon had returned home the day after Zeus had lain with his wife. The divine origin of Heracles, who possessed extraordinary, superhuman strength far surpassing that of his mortal brother Iphicles, was revealed at a very early age in **the episode of Hera's serpents**. And he continued throughout childhood to make show of his power. Like many young men of noble lineage, the brothers were sent to study letters and music with Linus. Iphicles was a docile and hard-working student whereas Heracles was inattentive and undisciplined; one day, when Linus had tried to correct his unruly pupil, Heracles struck him dead with his stool (or with his own his lyre, on which the teacher had made him practice some fingering exercises

Gigantic and extraordinarily strong, Heracles has always personified superhuman strength. Colossal statue of Heracles, known as the Farnese Hercules *(2nd cent. AD), from the Baths of Caracalla in Rome.* Naples, National Archaeological Museum.

Heracles' Troubled Early Life

Even before his birth, Heracles was the victim of Hera's jealousy. Zeus had boasted that his son would rule over the race of Perseus, Heracles' ancestor on his mother's side. Hera, knowing that Heracles' cousin Eurystheus was expected in the same period as he, then prevailed upon Zeus to swear that the first descendent of Perseus to be born would reign over Tiryns and Mycenae, in Argolis. Thereupon she called on her daughter Eileithyia, goddess of childbirth, to delay Alcmena's coming to term until the end of the tenth month and to anticipate the birth Eurystheus, who was born after only seven months and thus robbed Heracles of the empire Zeus had intended for him. Later, when Heracles was eight months old, Hera went to far as to make an attempt on his life. While Heracles and his twin Iphicles were asleep, she placed two enormous snakes in their cradle beside them; the snakes began to entwine themselves about the infants, to crush them. The terrified screams of Iphicles awoke Amphitryon, who ran to the cradle with his sword bared—only to find that Heracles had already strangled the snakes with his bare hands.

A curious fresco of the child Heracles strangling the serpents sent by Hera and so revealing his extraordinary strength to the incredulous onlookers.
House of the Vettii, Pompeii.

that he found uncongenial). Accused of murder, Heracles was tried and acquitted after having quoted a sentence by the hero of Crete and son of Zeus Rhadamanthys, who was renowned for his wisdom and equity. By this time, however, Amphitryon had become afraid of his foster son's intemperate behavior and determined to send him away from court to the country to tend cattle. The young hero's education was thus continued by a cowherd, a Scythian by the name of Teutarus, who taught Heracles the skills of archery; other versions cite other masters (Rhadamanthys himself, Eumolpus, and others) who taught him to wield arms and perfected his musical training.

At the age of just eighteen, Heracles performed the first of his heroic feats when he killed the lion of Mount Cithaeron, a monstrous and invincible beast that decimated Amphitryon's herds. No hunter before Hercules had dared attempt to rid the country of this ferocious creature.

On his way back to Thebes, Heracles met ambassadors from the king of Orchomenos, who were also bound for the city to collect the tributes owed to their king. Heracles attacked them, cut off their noses and ears, and hung them about their necks, saying that these were the tributes of Thebes. In the ensuing war waged by Orchomenos against Thebes Heracles fought beside his foster father Amphitryon who, although mortally wounded in battle, led his men to victory. Creon rewarded Heracles for aid to Thebes during the war with the hand of his daughter Megara, who bore Heracles numerous offspring. After some years Heracles once again incurred Hera's wrath and she sent a fit of madness upon him so that he killed his own children. Hera's plan was to force Heracles into the service of his cousin Eurystheus, to whom he was formally subject by virtue of the unhappy prophecy made by Zeus, and since Heracles' horrendous crime had left him tainted and impure, he determined with good grace to accept any sort of expiation. This was the scenario for the twelve Labors of Heracles (the Dodekathlon), which the hero was forced to perform; the Labors were ordered by Eurystheus, king of Tiryns and Mycenae, but were, as usual, inspired by Hera.

Left, a vigorous Heracles strangles the Nemean lion. Roman copy (1st-2nd cent. AD) of the original bronze group by Lysippus, one in a series of pieces depicting the Twelve Labors created for the city of Alyzia in Acarnania. Saint Petersburg, Hermitage. *Bottom, a Greek bronze statuette of a beardless young Heracles (4th cent. BC).* Vienna, Kunsthistorisches Museum.

The Dodekathlon (The Twelve Labors of Heracles)

The cycle of Heracles' Labors, formed over time from a rich epic tradition documented at least as far back as the 8th century BC but certainly based on an even older popular tradition, finally settled on a constant number (twelve) only when the complete series was represented in the twelve metopes (carved stone panels alternating with triglyphs, which make up the frieze) of the great Temple of Zeus at Olympia, built in about 460 BC. The difficulties faced by Heracles in the Dodekathlon, in which he was unceasingly aided by his young nephew and charioteer Iolaus and above all by the suggestions offered by his wise protectress, the goddess Athena, made him, more than any other classical hero, into an ideal figure: the personification of the heights attainable by man through moral fortitude and physical prowess. Thus, Heracles won out over every demonical and monstrous challenge sent his way, even in defiance of the power of the Underworld. The completion of the Labors even earned Heracles a place on Mount Olympus, where he lived eternally in the company of the gods.

The Nemean Lion

Despite a certain variation in the order of the Labors in different sources, it is generally agreed that the slaying of the enormous, ferocious lion that terrorized the plain of Nemea was the first. The lion was the son of the monster Echidna (the Viper with the body of a woman and a serpent's tail), and brother to the Theban Sphinx. Heracles attacked the beast first with a volley of arrows, then with his club and sword—but the bronze blade bent at the first blow. Realizing that the lion could not be slain with traditional weapons, Heracles approached him unarmed and, after a fierce struggle, strangled him. A further surprise came when Heracles discovered that even in death the animal's skin was impossible to cut (according to Theocritus it could be harmed "neither by iron or by fire"). To skin the beast a stratagem was called for: perhaps at Athena's suggestion, he used the mighty claws to rip the skin and of it made himself an invulnerable suit of armor; by forcing open the lion's jaws and inserting his head, he also procured himself an invincible helmet. From that moment on, Heracles's fundamental attribute was the pelt of the Nemean lion, with its teeth crowning his forehead and its huge clawed paws knotted over his chest.

Top, Heracles in his victorious struggle with the Hydra of Lerna. Marble relief (2nd cent. BC) from Lerna. Athens, National Archaeological Museum.

Bottom, Heracles defeating the Hydra painted in oil tempera on wood by Antonio del Pollaiolo (1475). Florence, Uffizi.

The Hydra of Lerna

Another child of Echidna, the terrifying Hydra, was a monster with the body of a serpent and many heads (the number varies, but is traditionally set at nine). It lived in the swamps near the ancient city of Lerna, preying on the herds and destroying crops and killing the region's inhabitants with stench of its breath alone. Heracles valiantly attacked the monster, but soon realized that no sooner had one head been dispatched than another grew in its place. The combat was further complicated by the appearance of a giant crab, sent by Hera, that fettered the hero's feet. Heracles was forced to ask the help of Iolaus, his charioteer and faithful companion in his Labors. They set fire to the nearby forest, and as Heracles struck off the heads with a razor-sharp scythe Iolaus, with the burning tree trunks, cauterized the stumps of the necks to prevent their regrowth. At the same time, Heracles crushed Hera's ferocious giant crab and so returned, again victorious, to Mycenae.

The Erymanthian Boar

The third Labor imposed on Heracles by king Eurystheus was to capture the enormous savage boar that lived on Mount Erymanthus in Arcadia, and bring it to Mycenae. Having discovered its lair, Heracles drove the boar into the open with loud shouts and chased it across the snow-covered mountains of the region until it was tired out; he then snared it, slung it over his shoulders, and carried it back alive to court at Mycenae. At the sight of the monstrous boar that Heracles was bringing to him, the terrified Eurystheus dived head first into one of the jars buried in the ground near his throne room, and from his hiding-place implored Heracles to take away the dreadful monster.

Heracles, having captured the fierce boar that rampaged on Mount Erymanthus, carries it on his back to the court of Eurystheus.
Marble votive relief (early 5th cent. BC).
Athens, National Archaeological Museum.

The Sad Story of the Centaur Pholus

The Centaurs, legendary beings with the body and legs of a horse but the torso, arms, and head of a man, appear—and often are presented in an extremely favorable light (for example, Achilles' wise mentor Chiron)—in many of the Greek myths. In the case of Heracles, tradition has it that after his exhausting chase of the Erymanthian boar, he rested for a time with his faithful friend Pholus, a good Centaur who lived in a cave and fed on the raw meat of the animals he hunted. Heracles was welcomed warmly by Pholus, who roasted meat especially for him, but when Heracles asked to have wine with his food Pholus replied that he had only one jar and that in any case it was the common property of all the Centaurs of the mountains. But Heracles insisted and Pholus finally bowed to the wishes of his friend, opened the jar, and served him the intoxicating wine. As its powerful aroma filled the surrounding woods, the other Centaurs flocked to the cave and besieged it in a fury, attacking Heracles. In the confusion, the worst lot fell to Pholus, who died after having accidentally wounded himself with one of the poisoned arrows that Hercules had tipped with the blood of the Hydra.

Heracles and Pholus open the jar of wine belonging to all the Centaurs, who respond furiously to the theft. Drawing after a red-figure Attic cup (500 BC). Basel, Basel Museum of Ancient Art.

The Cerynitian Hind

The fourth of the hero's Labors was to capture the hind of Cerynaia, larger than any stag, which although female and therefore by nature hornless bore golden horns. It was one of a herd of five that the goddess Artemis had found while she was out hunting; she caught four to draw her chariot, but the fifth ran free to Mount Cerynaia on the border of Argolis and Arcadia. Heracles chased the creature, whose speed was as unnatural as its aspect, for an entire year (one tradition has it that the hunt took him to the far-off north, through Istria and to the land of the Hyperboreans). Finally tired out, the magical hind stopped to rest by a river and Heracles was able to capture it after having inflicted a slight wound with one of his arrows. With the hind slung over his shoulders, he began his return journey to the court of Eurystheus with satisfaction—but was met along the way by Artemis and her divine twin Apollo, who sought to reclaim the hind as the property of the goddess of the hunt and even accused Heracles of having attempted to slay an animal sacred to the goddess and thus of having committed sacrilege. Heracles defended himself, pleading that he had been compelled to the Labor by Eurystheus; Apollo and Artemis, convinced of his innocent intent, allowed him to keep the captured hind and continue his journey.

Heracles attacks the magic golden-horned hind that ran wild on Mount Cerynaia. The enormous, swift, and powerful beast was sacred to Artemis, but she forgave Heracles for capturing it when she learned he was compelled to perform this Labor by Eurystheus. Marble metope from the Athenian Treasury at Delphi (shortly after 490 BC). Delphi, Archaeological Museum.

The Stymphalian Birds

In a thick, dark forest behind the marshes of **lake Stymphalis** in Arcadia there lived an enormous flock of birds that had originally hidden there to escape an invasion of wolves. They multiplied at an extraordinary rate, and had wonderful variegated feathers so sharply pointed that they speared to death any who came near them. They were a great plague on the entire land, since besides devastating crops they killed and devoured the local inhabitants. Eurystheus did not hesitate in send-

In obedience to Eurystheus, Heracles massacres the fearsome birds of Lake Stymphalus. Illustration from a Greek vase in the museum of Boulogne-sur-Mer. Paris, Decorative Arts Library.

Lake Stymphalis

Today, the mythical lake Stymphalis (Zaraka), round which in antiquity it seems there hung an air of dispiriting gloom, is no more than a small, insignificant pool due to the large-scale drainage, water management, and reclamation schemes that since ancient times have absorbed the energies of the inhabitants of this area of Arcadia. Long ago, Stymphalis was a true lake that faded into marshlands and was surrounded and protected by thickly-growing forests. For mythological tradition, the intricately entwined growth of these impenetrable woods suggested the lake as the ideal setting for the fierce and lethal flock of birds that was finally brought down by Heracles with the divine aid of Athena. History, instead, tells us that not far from the lakeside there stood the ancient Greek city of Stymphalus, which in the 4th century BC was ruled by the Arcadian League and later became a full member of the Achaean League.

ing Heracles to exterminate them. The hero immediately found himself faced with a practical problem: how to drive the huge flock from the tangled forest. It was Heracles' patroness and eternal ally Athena who devised the successful stratagem: she asked her faithful confederate Hephaestus, the god of fire, to forge a bronze clapper to startle the birds and force them to take flight. The unexpected and unusual noise indeed raised the birds in disorderly flight, and Heracles was thus able to pick them off with his arrows.

The Augean Stables

Augeas, son of Helios and king of Elis (the region of the great sanctuary of Zeus at Olympia) had inherited enormous herds of cattle from his father; in the huge stables the dung inevitably piled up day after day: not only were the animals forced to live in unhealthful conditions but the surrounding countryside was deprived of valuable fertilizer to the point that the entire region was faced with the devastating prospect of total barrenness. When Eurystheus ordered Heracles to clean the stables as his sixth Labor, Augeas was delighted and even accepted the wager proposed by the hero: if Heracles succeeded in completing the task in one day, Augeas would present Heracles with the tenth part of his herds. Heracles breached the walls around the stable yard and diverted the waters of two nearby rivers, the Alpheus and the Peneus, through the stables and the yard, so washing all the filth away in the appointed time. But Augeas, irritated by Heracles' unexpected success, refused to pay his wager until Augeas' own son, the young and honest prince Phyleus, intervened to testify to the agreement and establish the truth and just settlement.

The Cretan Bull

Heracles' seventh Labor, the first accomplished outside the Peloponnese, took the hero to Crete to capture a ferocious bull of extraordinary strength. The traditions regarding the identification of this animal are in clear conflict: according to some, this was the same bull that galloped over the waves and carried Europa to the island (this version is favored by those who do not accept that Zeus himself transformed into a bull to seduce the lovely Europa); according to others, it was the fine beast that captivated Pasiphae, wife of King Minos, and sired the Minotaur; in a third version, it was a bull that miraculously emerged from the sea the day Minos promised to sacrifice to Poseidon whatever should appear on the waves. By this account, when Minos saw how perfect the bull was he decided to keep it as one of his own and to sacrifice a different bull to Poseidon. Enraged at the deceit, Poseidon made the bull mad and it began wreaking havoc and devastation throughout the island—until Heracles caught it with his lasso and carried it back alive to the court of Eurystheus. The king decided to consecrate it to Hera, but the goddess was reluctant to accept any offering made possible—and precious—by Heracles, whom she so strenuously opposed, and so released the bull to roam wild in Greece: it reached the plains of Marathon before it was finally recaptured by Theseus.

Steatite rhyton in the form of a bull's head, from Knossos, Crete (1550-1500 BC). The eye is rock crystal; the muzzle is outlined in mother of pearl; the horns were gilded during restoration. Herakleion, Archaeological Museum.

To tame the flesh-eating mares of Diomedes, Heracles had to overpower their master. While they fought, the beasts devoured the hero's young companion, Abderus, in whose memory Heracles founded the nearby city of Abdera. Drawing after the inside decoration of a black-figure on coral cup attributed to the great Athenian painter Psiax, also known as the Menon Painter (ca. 510 BC). Saint Petersburg, Hermitage.

The Horses of Diomedes

Diomedes, son of the god Ares, was king of the wild region of Thrace on the shores of the Black Sea. He kept four savage **mares** tethered with iron chains to a bronze manger and fed them the flesh of any unsuspecting visitor who chanced to cross into his kingdom. Heracles, ordered by Eurystheus perform the difficult Labor of taming these animals and leading them back to his court, traveled to distant Thrace where he captured Diomedes and let his own mares devour him; this was in fact the only way of making them docile. He was then able to lead them, with no further trouble, to Eurystheus' palace; the king dedicated them to Hera and set them free near Mycenae, where, it is said, the breed survived until the time of Alexander the Great.

The Girdle of Hippolyte

The bellicose Amazons, a people of female warriors who amputated their right breast that it should not interfere with their archery or throwing the javelin, so nursing their infants (although only girl-children were allowed to live) only from the left, lived in the distant and mysterious lands of the north on the slopes of the Caucasus, with Themiscyra as their capital. Their valorous, queen Hippolyte, daughter of Ares, had been given a precious girdle by her father as a symbol of her absolute power over her people. Eurystheus' daughter Admete

Heracles fighting with Diomedes, king of Thrace and son of Ares. Marble sculptural group by Vincenzo de' Rossi (16th cent.). Florence, Palazzo Vecchio, Salone dei Cinquecento.

Diomedes' Mares in Legend

Diomedes' ferocious horses certainly struck a chord with the ancient imagination, since there grew up around them an entire and elaborate series of traditions, all relating the same episode in different manners. One of these, not too widely accepted, narrates how Heracles was sent to Thrace not alone but accompanied by a group of volunteers, in consideration of the extremely perilous nature of the task set him; one of the party was the young Abderus, of whom Heracles was particularly fond. The hero had little trouble capturing the mares, but when attacked by Diomedes and his troops he was forced to leave Abderus to mind the animals, which devoured their young and inexperienced keeper. After having killed Diomedes and fed him to the mares, which thereupon became tame, Heracles provided that Abderus be given a fitting burial and founded the city of Abdera on the site of his tomb.

coveted the girdle and so . . . The hero armed a ship and set sail with several volunteers, among whom Theseus and Telamon. When they reached Themiscyra at the mouth of the river Thermodon, the heroes were welcomed by the Amazons, and Hippolyte would willingly have yielded her girdle to Heracles had not the jealous Hera sewn the seeds of discord: in the guise of an Amazon, she infiltrated the ranks of the warriors and spread the rumor that Heracles and the others had come to kidnap Hippolyte. The fierce battle that ensued concluded with the death of Hippolyte by the hand of Heracles, who then completed his ninth Labor by removing the girdle from her body and carrying it back to Admete.

The First Trojan War

As tradition has it, it was during Heracles' return journey after having procured Hippolyte's girdle that the so-called First Trojan War broke out. Laomedon, then king of Troy, offended the gods Apollo and Poseidon, who were helping him build the city, by first promising to give them the marvelous horses he had earlier received as a gift from Zeus in exchange for their aid and then, after completion of the construction of the city walls, the finest ever seen, reneging on his promise. Poseidon sent a sea-monster against Troy, and Apollo a pestilence. These terrible plagues could be made to cease only if Laomedon's daughter Hesione were sacrificed to the sea-monster. Heracles happened to arrive at Troy in time to slay the monster and save the beautiful maiden, who he then gave in marriage to Telamon, his friend and companion-at-arms in the engagement with the Amazons.
As punishment, Hercules killed Laomedon and all his sons except, at Hesione's beseeching, the youngest, named Podarces ("swift-footed"). In exchange, Hesione offered the hero a veil which she herself had embroidered with gold. From that time on, the young prince was called Priam (from the Greek verb *priami*, meaning "buy free" or "franchise") and later on became the most famous of all the kings of Troy.

The Amazons were a population of female warriors and excellent horsewomen who, according to tradition, lived in the far-off Caucasus region. Detail of a Greek red-figure vase (4th cent. BC). Naples, National Archaeological Museum.

The Cattle of Geryon

Heracles in combat with the three-bodied monster Geryon. Drawing after an embossed bronze shield band (ca. 550 BC) from the sanctuary of Zeus at Olympia. Olympia, Archaeological Museum.

Geryon, the monstrous son of Chrysaor and therefore nephew to the Gorgon, was a three-bodied warrior who lived on the island of Erytheia at the western edge of the world. He owned enormous herds of cattle, tended by the herdsman Eurytion and the watchdog Orthrus. Eurystheus ordered Heracles to capture the cattle and to kill both their guardians and their owner.

The difficulties posed by this tenth Labor were considerable, the first problem being the crossing of Ocean. Hercules decided to procure for his voyage the Sun's golden urn, a huge hemispherical vessel on which the god embarked every evening to reach his home in the East of the world. As Heracles was crossing the Libyan desert, annoyed by the violent heat of the Sun, he drew his bow and began shooting his powerful arrows upward. The Sun protested and Heracles promised to shoot no more if the god would lend him his golden urn to sail to Erytheia. As he arrived on Geryon's island he was attacked by the dog Orthrus, which he killed with a blow of his club; Eurytion, who had run to the aid of his dog, was overcome by the hero's poisoned arrows; lastly, Heracles tackled Geryon himself, whose three bodies he dispatched one after the other. He then loaded the cattle into the Sun's golden urn and ferried them to the court of Eurystheus, who sacrificed the animals to Hera.

Black-figure Attic hydria painted by Lydos (ca. 560 BC). Rome, National Museum at Villa Giulia.

Heracles in the presence of his protectress, the goddess Athena, attempts to calm Cerberus, the fierce guardian of the Underworld, in order to capture him. Drawing after the red-figure Attic amphora decorated on both sides by the Andokides Painter (ca. 520 BC). Paris, Louvre.

Facing page, top, Heracles battles the sea-god Nereus in an attempt to force him to reveal the whereabouts of the garden of the Hesperides. Drawing after an embossed bronze shield band (ca. 550 BC) from the sanctuary of Zeus at Olympia. Olympia, Archaeological Museum.
Bottom, Heracles and Antaeus painted in oil tempera on wood by Antonio del Pollaiolo (1475). Florence, Uffizi.

The Capture of Cerberus

The eleventh Labor imposed on Heracles by Eurystheus was to descend to the **Underworld** and capture Cerberus, the monstrous dog that guarded the kingdom of the Dead to prevent the living from entering and, with even greater vigilance, the dead from leaving. Generally depicted with two or more heads, a snake's tail, and a ridge of snake heads down its back, Cerberus could never have been taken without the aid of the gods. Thus, after preliminary initiation into the Eleusinian Mysteries, which taught how to reach the Underworld safely after death, with the help of Hermes and Athena Heracles descended into Hades' realm. Hades granted him permission to take the terrible Cerberus to the land of the living if he could defeat the dog without using any weapon. Heracles wrestled the animal with his bare hands and succeeded in overpowering it. He brought the monster Mycenae, where Eurystheus was terrified at the sight of him, and, at a loss about what to do with his prize, asked Heracles to return the creature to the Underworld.

The Apples of the Hesperides

The last Labor of Heracles was to gather fruit from the golden apple-tree of the Hesperides, the Nymphs of the Evening. Hera had received some golden apples from Mother Earth (Gaia) on occasion of her marriage to Zeus, and she was so delighted with them that she planted them in her garden, near Mount Atlas at the western edge of the world and watched over by the Hesperides. But since the Nymphs, daughters of Atlas, were wont to secretly enter the garden and steal the magical fruit of the tree, Hera decided to have it guarded by Ladon, an immortal monster with one hundred heads, another son of Echidna. Heracles's greatest difficulty was to discover exactly where the garden lay; thus, he set out toward the sea. In Thessaly he fought and killed the brigand Cycnus, son of Ares, who murdered all passing travelers and offered their flesh in sacrifice to his father.

In Illyria, beside the waters of the river Erydanus, the hero met the River Nymphs, from whom he learned that only the sea-god Nereus would be able to direct him to the country he was searching for. He was led before Nereus, who refused to give him directions—whereupon he caught the old god in a vice-like grip, from which Nereus could not escape no matter what shape he assumed and was eventually forced to reveal the way to the garden of the Hesperides.

The Underworld

The kingdom of the Underworld, also known as Hades, appears solidly-footed in Greek historical/literary tradition in the time of Homer, when it was imagined as a uniformly dark subterranean realm accessed through frightening cracks in the earth. Later, its location was also hypothesized as being in the extreme West of the world, beyond Ocean, where the Sun's rays never reached. All the dead, the meritorious and the impure alike, were gathered here. Only with time did the milieu become better defined and acquire rivers, custodians, judges, and ferrymen; and in its progressing complexity came to include a portion reserved exclusively for the just, Elysium (or Elysian Fields), and another reserved for evil souls, Tartarus. Hades, the god of the Underworld, was the ruler of the dead, and only in extremely rare cases did he allow the living to enter his domain. One of the few so privileged was Heracles. During his stay he met Theseus and Pirithous, who had descended to the Underworld to try to lead Persephone back to Earth but were caught by Hades and, in punishment, chained to a rock; the hero freed Theseus, but Pirithous remained due to his arrogance.

Heracles, with his weapons laid aside, struggles with the giant Antaeus who can only be defeated if lifted barehanded from the earth (Gaia, his mother, from which he drew his strength). The combat is witnessed by Heracles' supporter Athena and by another divine figure, perhaps Gaia, who already bemoans the fate of Antaeus. Drawing after a black-figure hydria (ca. 510 BC). Museum of Boulogne-sur-Mer (France).

In Lybia, Heracles strangled the Giant Antaeus, son of Poseidon, who forced all travelers into combat and then adorned his father's temple with their battered remains.

Left, Heracles freeing the Titan Prometheus from his chains. Drawing after an Attic krater attributed to the Nessus Painter (ca. 610 BC). Athens, National Archaeological Museum.

In Egypt, instead, Heracles encountered the vilely cruel king Busiris, who put him in chains and was about to sacrifice him on an altar when Heracles burst his fetters, tore off the sacred bands, and slew Busiris and his attendants.
During his travels in the Caucasus, Heracles had liberated the Titan Prometheus from the torment inflicted on him by Zeus, who had chained him to the mountain where his eagle fed daily on his liver. In gratitude, Prometheus told Heracles not to take the apples from the Hesperides himself but to seek the help of his fellow Titan and brother Atlas.

Right, Heracles takes the burden of the heavens momentarily from the Titan Atlas, and in return Atlas fetches the magical apples from the garden of the Hesperides. Metope from the temple of Zeus at Olympia, carved by the Master of Olympia (ca. 460 BC). Olympia, Archaeological Museum.

Heracles kills Busiris and his Egyptian priests on the altar where they intended to sacrifice the hero. The Egyptians are easily recognizable as they are circumcised, and have shaven heads and Negroid features. Red-figure pelike by the Athenian painter usually known as the Pan Painter (ca. 460 BC). Athens, National Archaeological Museum.

Atlas had been sentenced by the gods to holding up the sky on his shoulders. When Heracles reached his destination, he went to Atlas and offered to (temporarily) relieve him of his burden while the Titan gathered three of the golden apples from the garden of the Hesperides for him. The task completed, Atlas refused to take back the firmament, saying he would take the apples to Eurystheus himself. Heracles feigned agreement but astutely asked Atlas to take the heavens back again for a moment while he arranged a cushion on his shoulders to better support the weight.
The unsuspecting Atlas was thus tricked into resuming his former role and Heracles was free to return to Mycenae. Eurystheus took the three apples, but beyond admiring their beauty he had no idea what to do with them and gave them back to Heracles, who in turn gave them to his constant advisor and supporter, Athena. The goddess returned them to the garden of the Hesperides, since divine law prohibited keeping such fruits anywhere else.

Love after Labor: Deianeira and the Story of Nessus

The lovely Deianera was the daughter of Oeneus king of Calydon. Her marriage to Heracles was prophesied by her ghost brother Meleager when Hercules descended to the Underworld—but he married her only after vanquishing another suitor, the river-god Achelous who appeared as a bull with a human face. Later, in exile from Calydon for having unwittingly killed one of Oeneus's relations, Heracles came with Deianeira to the banks of the Evenus, where the Centaur Nessus acted as ferryman. He took Heracles across and returned for Deianeira—but far from ferrying, he attempted to rape her. Heracles armed his powerful bow and shot Nessus. The dying Centaur plotted revenge: knowing that Heracles' arrows carried mortal poison, he told Deianeira to mix a love potion with the blood from his wound and to use it should Heracles ever fail in his love for her. Deianeira, suspecting no guile, made the potion. Some time later, Heracles became infatuated with Iole, daughter of Eurytus, king of Oechalia, and repudiated Deianeira. She remembered Nessus' promise and to win Heracles back dipped a tunic in the potion and gave it to him. But since the potion was tainted with the lethal poison of the blood of the Hydra in which Heracles had dipped his arrows, the hero fell into the throes of death. He begged all his followers to hasten his inevitable end.

The Apotheosis of Heracles: a Hero among the Gods

Only Philotectes resigned himself to obeying the hero. He built a tall pyre, placed Heracles on it, and set it alight. In recognition of Philotectes' comfortless fidelity, Heracles presented him with his bow and arrows. But as the fire caught, the heavens suddenly opened to reveal Athena on her chariot; she carried Hercules to Olympus, where he lived on with the immortal gods; after his reconciliation with Hera (partly in recognition of his role in the battle against the Giants) he received the gift of eternal youth from his father Zeus and was married to Hera's daughter Hebe, the cup-bearer of the gods.

In an alternate version of yhe myth, Heracles kills the Centaur Nessus, who has attempted to rape Heracles' wife Deianeira, by plunging his sword between his shoulders. Monumental black-figure Attic funerary amphora decorated by the Nessus Painter (ca. 600 BC). Athens, National Archaeological Museum.

Facing page, top, Athena conducts Heracles to Olympus and, bottom, the apotheosis of Heracles. Illustrations (published 1813) after an amphora found in Vulci (Italy) and a Greek vase, respectively. Both in the Monsieur de Lamberg Collection. Paris, Decorative Arts Library.

Jason, Medea, and the Adventures of the Argonauts

Phrixius and Helle

Athamas, son of the god of the wind Aeolus, had as his first wife Nephele ("cloud") who bore him two children, Phrixius ("pelting rain") and Helle ("bright light"). He later became infatuated with Ino, the beautiful daughter of Cadmus king of Thebes, and abandoned Nephele, who in revenge sent a terrible drought over the region. Ino, who hated her stepchildren, tried to persuade Athamas to sacrifice them in an attempt to placate the divine wrath manifest in the infliction of the drought. Nephele came to the aid of her children by giving them the magical golden ram she had received as a gift from Hermes. Riding it, Phrixius and Helle were therefore able to escape toward Colchis, the wild region to the east of the Euxine (the Black Sea). During the crossing, Helle fell into the sea (*pontos* in Greek) at the Dardanelles strait, which has also been known as the Hellespont ever since. Safe in Colchis, Phrixius sacrificed the ram to Zeus, the protector of fugitives, and hung the sparkling Golden Fleece in Ares' sacred wood, with a terrible dragon to watch over it.

The young Phrixius, son of Athamas and Nephele, flees from his stepmother Ino, who wanted to be rid of both Phrixius and his sister Helle. Phrixius and Helle escaped towards the Black Sea clinging to the fleece of a golden ram that was a gift to their mother from Hermes. Detail of a red-figure Attic pelike (ca. 460 BC). Athens, National Archaeological Museum.

Jason and Pelias

It was this same mythical Golden Fleece that Pelias, Jason's uncle, demanded of his nephew as proof of his worth as successor to the throne of Iolcus, which was in fact Jason's rightful inheritance from his father Aeson. After Pelias usurped Aeson, the infant Jason was brought up and educated far from court by the Centaur Chiron. He returned as a man to Iolcus, dressed extravagantly in a leopard skin and wearing only one sandal, while Pelias was officiating at a public sacrifice. Pelias failed to recognize his nephew but he was reminded of an ancient prophecy of his overthrow by a man with one sandal. He therefore challenged Jason to recover the Golden Fleece, confident that he would be killed in the attempt.

Jason sent a messenger throughout Greece to recruit volunteers from among the great heroes of his time, and he armed a ship, known as the Argo after its shipwright but also meaning "swift-sailing." The members of the expedition were thenceforth known as the Argonauts. Some of its crew were seers, whose task it became to sift and interpret the premonitory signs; the vessel too had the gift of prophesy, as its prow had been carved by Athena herself from the trunk of an oak tree of the wood sacred to

The Argonauts as imagined in a 19th century painting by Cesare dell'Acqua. Trieste (Italy), Castello di Miramare.

Zeus beside the god's great sanctuary at Dodona.
After many adventures (none of which, incidentally, is depicted in classical art) that took the ship and her heroic company to the shores of the most varied lands where they met many strange peoples, the Argonauts landed in Colchis. They were welcomed by king Aeètes, who was informed of Pelias's challenge and willing to surrender the Golden Fleece if Jason, alone, would yoke two fire-breathing, bronze-hoofed bulls and plow and sow a field with the teeth of a dragon.

Medea: Magic and Passion

It would naturally have been impossible for Jason to perform the tasks set him by Aeètes without the aid of the king's daughter, the witch-priestess **Medea**. She fell deeply in love with Jason and prepared for him a potion that made both his body and his weapons invincible to the attacks of the bulls—and she also warned Jason of her father's little secret: that warriors would miraculously rise from the dragon's teeth sown in the field. She also told him how to defeat them by throwing a stone quoit to set them fighting one against the other in fatal combat. Jason promised Medea undying love and matrimony and they fled together, but not before Jason had snatched the Golden Fleece. Aeètes followed in desperate pursuit, but he was forced to stop along the way to gather the limbs and recompose and bury the body of his young son Apsyrtus, killed and dismembered purposely by the boy's sister Medea to distract the king.

The goddess Athena intervenes to force the dragon guarding the Golden Fleece to regurgitate Jason. Drawing after the central tondo of a red-figure cup painted by the Athenian painter Douris (ca. 470 BC). Rome, Vatican Museums.

A Perfect Tragic Heroine

Medea, by some traditions the niece and by others the sister of Circe, and a witch herself, exhibits all the qualities of the perfect tragic heroine. Of passionate and volatile character, capable of love that can inspire any deed but at the same time pretends perfect fidelity, this young woman faces her sad destiny with courage and strength yet, again in the name of love, reveals herself possessed of incredible callousness and brutality—as when, in taking her revenge on Jason, she kills both her children by him, Mermerus and Pheres. Some traditions narrate how following this bitter event Medea ascended to the heavens; others, that a chariot drawn by winged dragons carried her to Athens where she then lived at length with king Aegeus. Medea, from Pindar's time onward inextricably linked to the doings of Jason, inspired many an ancient writer. It is from the *Medea* composed by Euripides in 431 BC, which focuses on the later, tragic events of her story, that the popularity of the heroine and the most common form of the myth derives; and it was this tragedy that inspired Apollonius Rhodius to write his *Argonautica* as well as such Latin authors as Ennius, Ovid, and Seneca. Nor must we forget more recent works, like that by Corneille or, in music, Niccolini, in whose operatic version Medea lives on in our day and continues to hold center stage as the perfect incarnation of the tragic heroine of ancient Greece, who not by chance was given a voice—and the face many immediately associate with the name—by Maria Callas in her unforgettable interpretation of the role.

Medea demonstrates her rejuvenating potion to the daughters of Pelias by boiling a ram in a large cauldron, and persuades them to try the same treatment on their father. Drawing after a black-figure Attic hydria (ca. 510 BC). London, British Museum.

Jason and the Golden Fleece in a 17th century painting by Erasmus Quellinus. Madrid, Prado.

Zeus, angered by the barbaric murder of Apsyrtus, hurled down a howling tempest that sent the Argo off course as it was returning home. The magical ship suddenly began to speak and revealed the origin of the storm and that it would not calm until the heroes had been purified by the witch Circe, Medea's own aunt. Circe performed the necessary purification but offered the travelers no hospitality. The ship then headed again for the open sea and visited the Strait of Messina, Sicily, Corfu, Crete, Aegina, and Euboea before finally returning home to Iolcus.
Delivering the Golden Fleece to Pelias did not, however, put an end to Jason's troubles, since the king refused to keep his promise to resign the throne. Once again it was Medea who helped the hero: she persuaded the daughters of Pelias that if they cut the king to pieces and boiled them in a large bronze cauldron together with one of her magic potions, he would be rise again with renewed youth and vitality. Of course he did not, but far from winning the throne Jason and Medea were forced to flee from Iolcus to Corinth to escape the vengeance of Pelias's son Acastus.
At Corinth, where Jason dedicated the ship Argo to Poseidon in his sanctuary on the isthmus, the hero fell in love with Glauce, daughter of King Creon, and repudiated Medea. To wreak her revenge Medea sent the bride a poisoned robe and diadem that caused her death the instant she tried them on.

This page, Theseus' aged and infirm mother Aethra was taken prisoner during the Trojan war and kept as a slave inside the city walls until Greeks ended the siege and took the city thanks to the wooden horse; Theseus' sons Acamas and Demophon led their grandmother to freedom. Drawing after a red-figure krater decorated by the Athenian painter Myson (ca. 500 BC). London, British Museum.

Jason, driven to madness by his loss, turned against Medea—but she acted more quickly, killing her two sons by Jason before retreating to the heavens in a wonderful chariot sent by the Sun.

Theseus, the Athenian hero

Although sometimes cited as the son of Poseidon, Theseus, the Athenian hero par excellence, was the son of Aegeus, king of Athens, and of Aethra, daughter of Pittheus, king of Troezen in the Peloponnese. Fearful for Theseus' safety in Athens, in the midst of his jealous cousins, the fifty sons of Pallas all of whom had designs on the throne, Aegeus and Aethra took the young Theseus to Troezen to be brought up in his grandfather's house. Before leaving on his return journey, Aegeus hid his sword and sandals under an enormous rock, telling only Aethra of their whereabouts and enjoining her to reveal the secret to Theseus only when he was strong enough to lift the rock and retrieve his father's gifts—and therefore return to Athens.

Theseus' Adventures on the Road to Athens

When it came time, Theseus left for Athens, but only after being warned by his mother Aethra and his grandfather Pittheus not to travel the land route, since Heracles, the Peloponnese's greatest hero, had been absent for some time and the roads were once again infested with brigands and monsters. Theseus was instead keen to emulate the fame of the hero and chose to journey on the infested highways rather than sail the safer seas.
At Epidaurus he met Hephaestus' deformed son Periphetes, who walked with a bronze club as a cane

Drawings after a red-figure cup showing the deeds of Theseus, decorated by the Athenian painter Douris (ca. 470 BC) and discovered at Vulci (Italy). Side A (top): on the left, Theseus attacking the Crommyum sow while Phea, the old woman who kept her, tries to restrain him, and on the right, Theseus punishing the brigand Sinis with the same torture Sinis had inflicted on others.
Side B (bottom): Theseus punishing the brigands Sciron and Cercyon in the presence of Athena. Sciron being thrown down from the cliff where he threw his victims after forcing them to wash his feet; Theseus wrestling and crushing Cercyon to death just as the Giant had crushed so many passers-by. London, British Museum.

that he also used to strike dead anyone who came near him. Theseus slew him and took possession of his club, which became his favorite weapon.
The hero then rid the isthmus of Corinth of the brigand Sinis by inflicting on him the same torture he had inflicted on so many travelers; that is, to waylay strangers and tie them to the tips of two pine trees bent down by force, which when released tore the victim in two.
In the forest near Crommyum, Theseus fought the fierce wild sow that destroyed crops and killed men in the region. She was thought to be one of the monstrous offspring of Typhon and Echidna, and therefore the sister of Cerberus, Orthrus, the Chimera, the Hydra of Lerna, the dragon that guarded the Golden Fleece, and the monster that watched over the apples in the garden of the Hesperides; she was also the half-sister of the Nemean lion, born of Echidna by her son Orthrus. Theseus killed the sow, called Phea after the old woman who kept her, with the sword left him by his father Aegeus under the rock at Troezen.
Near Scironea Saxa, on the narrow pass in the cliff road near Megara, Theseus came across the brigand Sciron, who preyed on travelers asking them to wash his feet and then, when they bent down to do so, kicking them into the sea below, where they were devoured by a giant turtle. Theseus treated Sciron in the same manner, so ridding the pass of this inhuman tribute.
Near Eleusis, not far from the border with Megaris, Theseus defeated the

Lively representations of some of the legendary exploits of Theseus during his long journey toward Athens adorn this Greek red-figure plate (ca. 440 BC). At the center, Theseus dragging the corpse of the Minotaur. From the bottom, clockwise, the brigand Sinis, on whom Theseus inflicted the same torture by which Sinis killed his victims, and the ferocious sow Phea, slain with the sword left Theseus by his father Aegeus, as Phea's guardian (of the same name) looks on. At the top, Theseus wrestling with the Giant Cercyon; the winner of the match, as of so many others, was the Athenian hero.

From top to bottom, the exploits of Theseus continue with the brigand Procrustes and the shorter of his famous beds of torture, on which Theseus killed him; the brigand Sciron, son of Poseidon, with the gigantic sea turtle that devoured his victims— and Sciron, when Theseus threw him into the sea; and Poseidon's savage white bull that Theseus succeeded in capturing and sacrificed to Apollo on the Athens Acropolis.

Giant Cercyon, son of Poseidon, who forced passers-by to wrestle him and then put them to death. Despite the marked difference in their size Theseus proved more skillful than his adversary and won out by lifting him above his head and sending him smashing to the ground, crushing him to death.

Continuing on the road from Megara to Athens, Theseus came to the house of Procrustes (also known as Damastes), who reserved a unique torture for strangers. He had two beds, one short and one long; tall travelers were forced to lie on the shorter bed and had their extremities trimmed to fit it, while shorter victims were racked to fit the longer bed. In this case too, Theseus dispatched the brigand by making him a victim to his own torture.

After such adventures, all faced courageously but ending in as many deaths, Theseus had to be purified by the priests on the banks of the river Cephissus in Attica before he could approach the palace of his father Aegeus in Athens. Here he did not reveal his identity immediately, since he had come to know that the king was under the magic power of Medea, who (according to some versions of the myth) had come to Athens from Corinth to escape the vengeance of Jason. Medea, who had recognized Theseus, devised a plan to be rid of him and so smooth the way to power for the fifty sons of Pallas, all of whom were eager to take over the government and seize the estate of Aegeus, whom they assumed to be without heirs. But just as Theseus was about to drink the potion Medea had prepared for him, Aegeus recognized the sword and sandals he had hidden in Troezen long ago and thus saved his son. He drove Medea from court and killed or exiled most of the cousins to eliminate them as threats to Theseus.

The Cretan Cycle

Theseus remained with his father, the undisputed sovereign of Athens. The city was oppressed by the heavy tribute imposed by Minos, king of Crete: every nine years the Athenians were required to send seven youths and seven maidens to be eaten by the monstrous son of Minos, the Minotaur, a man with the head of a bull who dwelt locked in the mythical labyrinth. Theseus volunteered to be numbered among those sent to Crete, with the intention of freeing his city from the shameful tribute. He promised his father that should his mission prove successful the returning ship would unfurl white sails,

Marble torso of the Minotaur slain by Theseus. Athens, National Archaeological Museum.

A gold stater coined in the city of Knossos in the 4th century BC, with an image of the labyrinth of the monstrous Minotaur. Theseus penetrated the labyrinth, killed the monster, and exited following Ariadne's thread. Rethymnon, Archaeological Museum.

but otherwise it would raise the black sails used on the sorrowful outward journey.

On Crete, Aphrodite came to his aid by making Ariadne, Minos' lovely daughter, fall in love with him. Ariadne was strolling on the beach with her nurse when she saw the young Athenians led by Theseus and decided to help him by showing him how to find his way out of the labyrinth. She gave him a ball of wool, which he slowly unraveled as he penetrated the complicated maze of corridors that was the labyrinth; after having found the Minotaur and killed him with his sword he returned, rewinding the thread, to the princess, who was waiting anxiously outside the labyrinth.

Theseus fled to his ship with Ariadne, to whom he made false promises of love, and the company of young

Athenians who had escaped being sacrificed to the monster. On their way back to Athens they stopped on the island of Naxos, where Ariadne fell asleep on the beach. Theseus took advantage of the situation and took off again for home without her (other versions of the myth say a violent storm hastily drove the ship away from Naxos before Ariadne could embark). In either case, when Ariadne awoke and realized she had been abandoned she sank into despair; but she was soon distracted by the arrival of the festive procession of Dionysus, with the god riding on his magical chariot drawn by panthers. Dionysus fell in love with her as soon as he saw her and carried her away in his chariot to Mount Olympus, where he made her his bride and obtained the gift of immortality for her from Zeus. Meanwhile, Theseus had drawn close to Athens but, intoxicated by his success, forgot to unfurl the white sails as he had promised his father. Aegeus, who had kept watch every day for the return of the ship, saw the black sails in the distance and concluded that the mission had failed and that all the young Athenians and his own son had been sacrificed to the Minotaur. In despair, he threw himself into the sea from the Acropolis of Athens. Still today, the Aegean Sea bears his name, and at the foot of the walls supporting the

Theseus holds the Minotaur to the ground and prepares to inflict a mortal blow as the monster raises a hand as though imploring mercy. Red-figure Attic pelike (ca. 480 BC). Rome, Vatican Museums.

small temple of Athena Nike are two niches that traditionally recall his death, as they are said to be the site where the old king was worshiped.

Theseus' Reign in Athens

As lord of Athens and Attica, Theseus is remembered mainly for having united the various regions of Attica in a single community and as the founder of the Panathenaea, the great religious festival in honor of the goddess Athena in which all the inhabitants of Attica participated. The yearly celebrations were the occasion for contests, ceremonies, processions, parades, and races.

Late in life, since the political climate in the city had turned against him, Theseus resigned the throne of Athens to Menestheus and took refuge on the island of Scyros at the court of a relative of his, king Lycomedes. After having extended to Theseus an apparently warm welcome, Lycomedes led him to the top of a high hill, on the pretext of showing him the splendid view of the island, and threw him over the cliff to his death.

During the battle of Marathon (490 BC) in the war between the Greeks and the Persians, Athenian soldiers reported seeing a hero of magnificent stature who they recognized as Theseus fighting in their front ranks. At the end of the war the Athenian statesman Cimon consulted the Delphic oracle who ordered him to retrieve the bones of Theseus and bring them back to Athens. Cimon thus set out for Scyros and took the island. Having sighted upon his arrival an eagle scraping the earth with its talons at the top of the hill, he recognized it as an augury and excavated the spot, where he discovered a tomb containing the bones of a warrior, a bronze spear, and a sword. The bones of Theseus were brought back to Athens and feted in a manner worthy of a god.

After they had fled from Crete, Theseus and Ariadne rested on the island of Naxos, where Athena appeared to the hero in the dead of night and insisted that he return immediately to Athens. The unsuspecting Ariadne lies asleep with the small figure of Hypnos (Sleep) nestling above her head. Red-figure Attic lekythos (ca. 480 BC). Taranto (Italy), National Archaeological Museum.

The Minor Exploits of Theseus

To the much-loved Athenian hero Theseus, tradition attributes a host of trying exploits. Many of these stories are very well known, like that of the war against the Amazons. Theseus was powerfully attracted by the proud female warriors and journeyed, with Heracles, to their capital at Themiscyra. When they arrived, Theseus was warmly welcomed by the Amazon queen, who even sent one of her followers, Antiope, with precious gifts for the new guest.

According to one tradition, Theseus invited the beautiful Antiope—who is sometimes cited as the queen of the Amazons—to board his ship, and then set sail with his prey. The Amazons invaded Attica to recover her, advancing as far as Athens and engaging in bitter combat with the army led by Theseus. Theseus and his forces eventually put one wing of the Amazon army to flight so that the women were forced to make peace.

Antiope bore Theseus Hippolytus, but the hero then became infatuated with the lovely Phaedra, daughter of Minos and sister to Ariadne. In order to marry her Theseus repudiated Antiope—but he kept his young son Hippolytus, who grew strong and brave like his father.

His stepmother Phaedra fell in love with him, but when rebuffed she denounced him as her seducer and had him punished by Theseus. Theseus asked Poseidon to administer punishment: the god sent down a wild bull, which emerged unexpectedly from the waves and spooked the horses pulling Hippolytus' chariot; they then ran amok, dragging the youth to his death.

Theseus still had many heroic exploits before him, like the capture of a ferocious bull who breathed fire from his nostrils and ran wild in the plain of Marathon, destroying crops and attacking peasants (it has been said that this was the same bull Heracles brought from Crete to Eurystheus, who had consecrated it to Hera but then let it free).

Theseus abducting the Amazon queen Antiope. Greek amphora (5th cent. BC) found in Vulci (Italy). Paris, Louvre.

Perseus and Medusa

Acrisius, king of Argolis, had imprisoned his daughter Danae in an impenetrable subterranean bronze chamber in an attempt to prevent the fulfilment of a prophecy that he would be overthrown by his own grandson. Zeus, enamored of the maiden, succeeded in visiting her as a shower of gold—and so Danae conceived Perseus. The cries of the baby at birth alerted Acrisius, who placed mother and child in a wooden ark and abandoned them to the waves. After drifting here and there, the two were washed ashore on the island of Seriphos, were they were welcomed by king Polydectes. As Perseus grew he protected his mother from the advances of Polydectes and the king, to rid himself of Perseus and his unwelcome interference, charged him with the dangerous task of finding the hiding-place of the Gorgons and of killing the only mortal among them, Medusa. Perseus received the help of both Hermes and Athena, who suggested stratagems and gave him miraculous devices to

Perseus, in the presence of his protectress Athena, decapitates the Gorgon, turning his head away to avoid being turned into stone. The blood from the Gorgon's head has already given birth to one of her children, Pegasus, the winged horse, but Chrysaor is not yet born. Limestone metope (ca. 530 BC) from Selinunte in Sicily (ancient Selinus). Palermo (Italy), National Archaeological Museum.

The severed head of the Medusa, roiling with serpents, in all the tragic expressiveness of Caravaggio's famous painting (after 1590). Florence, Uffizi.

ensure his success: winged sandals for a swift retreat, a sack to carry the evil head of the Medusa, and a helmet that made him invisible.

Perseus then sought out the Graeae, the three sisters of the Gorgons. They were hideous in appearance, having been born old; among them, they had only one tooth for eating and one eye for seeing, which they used in turns. Perseus managed to snatch the eye from them and used it to blackmail the Graeae into revealing the whereabouts of the grotto where the Gorgons hid.

When Perseus reached the hideaway of the three Gorgons (Stheno, Euryale, and Medusa), he found them asleep. The sisters were monsters, with necks covered in dragon scales, tusks like those of the wild boar, brazen hands, and golden wings—but most fearsome of all were their locks of writhing serpents. They also had the power to petrify anyone who caught their eye. To aid Perseus, Athena held up her polished bronze shield so that the hero could follow Medusa's reflected movements without risking her direct gaze. Perseus thus succeeded in decapitating the Gorgon; he placed her head in the bag, put on his helmet, and, invisible, took flight immediately to escape the wrath of the other two, immortal, sisters. As he left the cave and fled to safety, two streams of blood flowed copiously from the Medusa's head: the left, malign spurt was lethal poison while the right, benign spurt, was collected by Athena and given to Asclepias, who

used it to cure the sick and even to resuscitate the dead. The blood shed by Medusa also gave birth to her children, the winged horse Pegasus, later tamed by Bellerophon to fight against the Chimera, and the warrior Chrysaor, the "youth with the golden sword." Perseus later gave Medusa's head to Athena, who wore it on her aegis, the armor made of the invulnerable skin of the goat Amalthea.

On his way home with his trophy Perseus spied a girl of wondrous beauty in mortal peril, and saved her. She was Andromeda, daughter of Cepheus and Cassiopeia, the rulers of Ethiopia. As Cassiopeia had offended the Nereids (the Sea Nymphs) Poseidon had sent a sea **monster** to devastate the coasts of Ethiopia, promising an end to the plague if Andromeda were sacrificed to the monster; the young princess was thus chained to the rocks to await the appearance of the sea-monster, which would have devoured her as his sacrificial victim had not Perseus seen her and fallen in love with her. He promised her father Cepheus to battle the monster if he were granted Andromeda's hand in marriage. And so it was.

Facing page, top, the courageous Perseus freeing Andromeda, in a small painting by Domenico Fetti, originally made as a furniture decoration (ca. 1621). Vienna, Kunsthistorisches Museum.
Bottom, a "knightly" champion kills the dragon before a crowd of onlookers in Piero di Cosimo's extremely elaborate, Gothic-style representation of the mythical episode of Andromeda being freed by Perseus (ca. 1515). Florence, Uffizi.

Right, Benvenuto Cellini's incomparable Perseus straddling the body of the Medusa and brandishing the severed head in triumph (1545-1554). Florence, Loggia dei Lanzi.

A World of Monsters

Mythology in general, and older myths in particular, are literally overrun with monsters and fantastic and imaginary beasts, which are often syntheses of other animals that really existed. The winged horse Pegasus, the Chimaera, the Sirens, and the Medusa are all excellent examples, but so are relatively "recent" creatures like the unicorn of medieval and Renaissance fame. Quite often, these beings not only represented an expression of lively imagination but provided concrete images that aided in the attempt to explain natural phenomena that otherwise would have been incomprehensible (for instance, a maelstrom) or catered to man's need to represent his greatest aspirations; for example, the atavistic desire to fly. How profoundly these creatures are linked to man's very nature is manifestly apparent in the way they continue to exert an irresistible fascination even in our times, and in how "modernized" versions of some of their number have become the protagonists of famous and well-loved fables.

Etruscan gilt clasp decorated with the winged horse Pegasus (ca. 530 BC). Rome, National Museum at Villa Giulia.

Bellerophon and the Chimaera

Bellerophon, son of Glaucus, king of Corinth, had involuntarily killed a man by the name of Bellerus, perhaps a tyrant of Corinth (hence the hero's name, "killer of Bellerus"). To expiate his crime Bellerophon was forced to go into exile, and at the court of King Proetus, in Tiryns, he was purified. The king's wife Stheneboea was strongly attracted to the handsome and noble appearance of the youth, but Bellerophon rejected her out of loyalty to the king. Feeling herself humiliated, Stheneboea took revenge by making Proetus believe that Bellerophon had attempted to seduce her. Proetus thus decided to send the hero to the court of Iobates, Stheneboea's father, in Lycia, to deliver a letter to him; unknown to Bellerophon, the message enjoined the king to put its bearer to death. Iobates was thus forced to excogitate a system for eliminating Bellerophon and decided to set for him the seemingly impossible task of killing the Chimaera. This monster, the daughter of Typhon and Echidna ("the viper") had the head and body of a lion—from which there also grew a fire-spitting goat's head—and a serpent in place of its tail. Bellerophon called on Athena for aid; the goddess presented him with a magic bridle with which to capture and tame the winged horse Pegasus, son of Medusa, as it drank at the Peirene spring in Corinth; flying high astride Pegasus, Bellerophon succeeded in escaping the mortal blows of the Chimaera's head and in killing her. Another version recounts how with his spear Bellerophon thrust a lump of lead into mouth of the goat-head; as it melted in the flames, the metal consumed the monster's entrails and killed her.

Bellerophon flying astride the magical Pegasus. Fragment of a terracotta antefix (ca. 540-500 BC). Thasos, Archaeological Museum.

The so-called "Chimaera of Arezzo," a magnificent bronze figure (5th cent. BC). Florence, Archaeological Museum.

Meleager, Atalanta, and the Calydonian Boar

Oeneus, king of the city of Calydon in Aetolia, had enjoyed a particularly abundant harvest and as a sign of his gratitude had made sacrificial offerings to all the gods—but by an oversight had omitted Artemis. The goddess took revenge by sending an enormous boar to devastate the land and kill the people. Meleager, the king's son by queen Althaia, decided to organize a hunt for the boar and so mustered the noblest heroes from throughout Greece in his aid: besides the Dioscuri (Castor and Polydeuces), Theseus, Jason, Iphicles, Pirithous, Telamon, Peleus, Amphiaraus, and others, he also summoned Atalanta, the only woman allowed to participate in those heroic and sporting activities generally reserved for men. Atalanta, who was born in Arcadia, had grown up excelling in all sports and even refused to marry anyone unable to defeat her in a running race—which she always won. Only Melanion, helped by Aphrodite, who had given him a few of the golden apples from the garden of the Hesperides, ever succeeded in winning. Melanion let fall the apples as he ran and Atalanta stopped to gather them, giving Melanion the edge he needed to win the race and take her as his bride. Atalanta was nevertheless accorded a heroic standing equal to that of any man by virtue of her defeat of so many rivals. Before leaving for the chase, Meleager had promised to give the head and skin of the boar to his mother Althaia on his return, so sure was he of success, but having fallen in love with Atalanta it was to her he presented the prize when the hunt was over. Slighted, Althaia sought revenge. When Meleager was born she had been presented with a burning brand by the Moirae, the goddesses that spin the threads of fate, with the promise that the child would live until the wood was entirely consumed. At the time, she had extinguished the flame and hidden the brand secretly. In her anger at her son's treachery she took up the stick from its hiding place and threw it on the fire where it quickly burned away and the unsuspecting Meleager died in an instant. His sisters cried and lamented his death so piteously that Artemis was moved and transformed them into birds, called *meleagrides* (guinea-fowl) by the ancient Greeks.

The statues of the Dioscuri (top and right) that since 1585 adorn the great balustrade of Piazza del Campidoglio *in Rome. They were moved there from their Roman temple of origin as part of Michelangelo's plan for restructuring the area.*

Bottom, Meleager and Atalanta, together with the noblest heroes in Greece, take part in the hunt of the fierce Calydonian Boar. Detail of a 2nd century AD Roman sarcophagus showing the boar wounding the hero Ancaeus, one of the Argonauts.

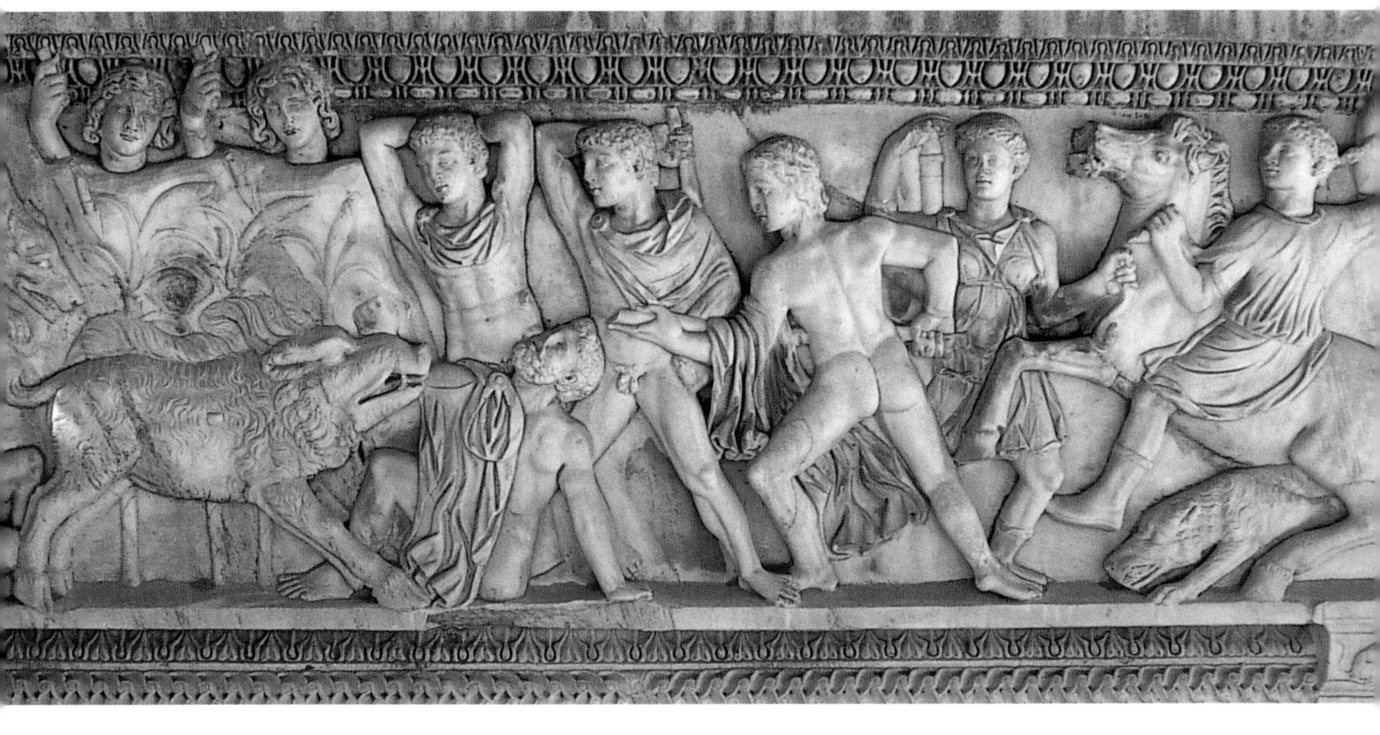

Oedipus, the Sphinx, and Ineluctable Destiny

Laius, king of Thebes of the Seven Gates, had been informed by an oracle that he would die by the hand of his own son, and so when his wife Jocasta bore him a child Laius ordered that the infant be taken from the city and put to death. However, the servant given the thankless task was unable to bring himself to kill the child. Instead, he left him exposed on Mount Cithaeron with his feet bound together and reported to the king and the court that he had indeed killed him. Periboea (or Merope), queen of Corinth and wife of Polybus, who was passing through the land near Thebes, noticed the child with his bound—and swollen—feet (hence his name, **Oedipus**); she took him in and brought him up as her own. Eventually Oedipus was informed, also by an oracle, that his destiny was to kill his own father. Horrified at this idea but unaware that he was not the true son of Polybus, Oedipus fled to Thebes, where on a narrow stretch of road he ran into Laius in his chariot and was ordered by the royal charioteer to stand aside. In the violent exchange that followed Oedipus killed both Laius and his charioteer. He continued on toward Thebes, ignorant of having fulfilled the prophecy,

Oedipus is asked a mysterious riddle by the Sphinx at the gates of Thebes. Inside of a red-figure Attic cup by the Oedipus Painter (his name-piece) (ca. 480 BC). Rome, Vatican Museums.

Facing page, Oedipus as he solves the Sphinx's riddle, in a painting by Jean Auguste Dominique Ingres (1808). Paris, Louvre.

The Tragic Myth of Oedipus

Oedipus, the hero of the Theban cycle, who through no fault of his own fell victim to a cruel destiny that led him to commit grievous acts and suffer their dramatic consequences, was a perfect model for ancient tragedy.
As protagonist of Cinaethone's epic cycle the *Oedipodea*, today lost but the source of all the later ancient works, and a character well known to Homer, Oedipus and his doings were at the center of many famous tragedies, like *Oedipus Tyrannus* and *Oedipus at Colonus* by Sophocles (5th century BC) and Euripides' *Phoenician Women*. In the modern era, the myth of Oedipus inspired celebrated literary figures from Corneille to Voltaire, and even Sigmund Freud had recourse to the old king when he coined the expression "Oedipus complex" to describe the love felt by young children for the parent of opposite sex and their rivalry with the other.

INGRES
1808

and stopped at the city gates, where he met the Sphinx. The monstrous creature, with the body of a lion and the head of a woman, challenged passers-by with a mysterious riddle and devoured those who were unable to solve it. Her question was, "What is it that walks on four legs in the morning, on two at noon, and on three in the evening?"
Oedipus understood the metaphor and gave the correct answer: "A man," who crawls when an infant, walks upright in his prime, and in old age requires the help of a stick. The defeated Sphinx hurled herself from the high rocks where she had perched for so long and died.
Upon entering Thebes the young man was met with a triumphant welcome from its citizens, who had for so long been harassed by the monster; he was also greeted enthusiastically at court and given the queen Jocasta, actually his mother, in marriage. After many years and the birth of four children, Antigone, Ismene, Eteocles, and Polyneices, a terrible plague descended on the city. The cause, according to the blind sage Teiresias, was the immoral, sinful conduct of the royal family. After careful enquiry, Oedipus discovered the true story of his life; Jocasta committed suicide and Oedipus blinded himself before quitting the city to wander as an exile in the sole company of his young daughter Antigone.

The Sphinx of Naxos, a stone votive statue on a high column in the sanctuary of Apollo at Delphi, dedicated by the inhabitants of the island of Naxos in ca. 570 BC. Delphi, Archaeological Museum.

Tydeus slays Oedipus' daughter Ismene, while Periclymenus escapes. Black-figure Corinthian amphora (ca. 560 BC). Paris, Louvre.

The Dramatic Consequences of Oedipus' Sins

The terrible sin committed by Oedipus, in perfect good faith, had terrible repercussions for all his descendants for generations. After the disappearance of their father, Eteocles and Polyneices fought ferociously for the throne. Polyneices' exile sparked a war in which six of Greece's major heroes sided with him and six with his brother, paired off at the city gates in the story known as *The Seven against Thebes*. At the end of the war the brothers killed each other. The legitimate successors of Oedipus having thus been eliminated, the throne passed to Jocasta's brother Creon, who gave Eteocles a fitting burial but denied the same honor to Polyneices and prohibited all and sundry, on pain of death, from performing the office. Antigone, after long and tormented debate over whether to obey divine or human law, gave symbolic burial to her brother by throwing a handful of earth on the body—and thus decreed her own death. Ismene fell in love with a young Theban; having arranged to meet with him near a spring, she was spied on and slain by the violent Tydeus.

CHAPTER IV

THE ILIAD: THE TROJAN WAR

THE HOMERIC DEBATE

Even though the historical figure of Homer is shrouded in legend, it is certain that between the 9th and the 7th centuries BC there existed, in the Greek world, a poet to whom we owe the composition of the Iliad *and the* Odyssey, *the two poems unanimously considered as marking the beginning of European literature.*
Legend tells us that Homer was blind, and many cities claim him as their son: Chios, Smyrna, Colophon, Pylos, and Athens.
The probable truth of the matter is that Homer was an aedo, a bard who wrote down—or had written for him—and then edited and improved on the enormous quantity of lyrics and poems that had been passed down orally through the preceding centuries. Aristarchus of Samothrace was the first to attribute the two epic poems the Iliad *and the* Odyssey *to Homer. The two differ as to form, but closely resemble each other in their styles of composition, structure, and narrative breadth.*
In the 3rd century BC, the so-called Alexandrian scholars came to the conclusion that the Iliad, *so impetuous and*

A marble head of Homer, of proud bearing despite his blindness, his face framed by a flowing beard, who immortalized the glorious Greek heroes. Rome, Capitoline Museums.

The apotheosis of Homer as imagined in the 1800's by Paul and Raymond Balze: the greatest of epic poets being crowned under the admiring gaze of the most eminent artists and thinkers of all time. Paris, Louvre.

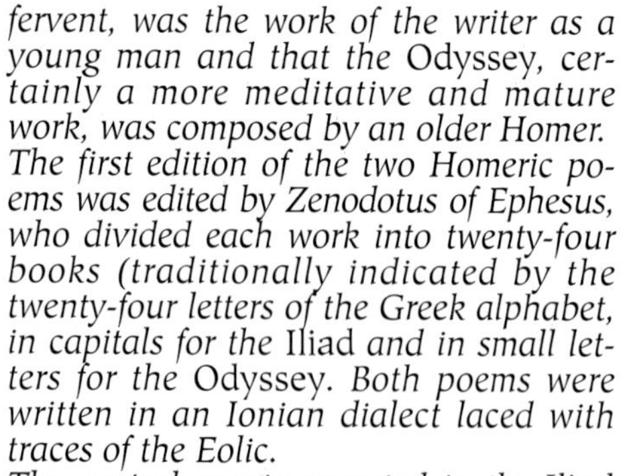

fervent, was the work of the writer as a young man and that the Odyssey, *certainly a more meditative and mature work, was composed by an older Homer. The first edition of the two Homeric poems was edited by Zenodotus of Ephesus, who divided each work into twenty-four books (traditionally indicated by the twenty-four letters of the Greek alphabet, in capitals for the* Iliad *and in small letters for the* Odyssey. *Both poems were written in an Ionian dialect laced with traces of the Eolic.*
The central events narrated in the Iliad *take place over the course of fifty-one days in the tenth and last year of the Siege of Troy; those of the* Odyssey, *over the course of forty-one days in the tenth and last year of Odysseus' wanderings, even though, through the device of the story told by Odysseus to Alcinous, the previous nine years' adventures are narrated as well.*

ΑΝΔΡΩΝ ΗΡΩΩΝ
ΚΟΣΜΗΤΟΡΙ

WHAT WENT BEFORE

THE MARRIAGE OF PELEUS AND THETIS

From the union of Peleus, king of Phthia in Thessaly, and the Sea Nymph Thetis (daughter of Nereus and therefore one of the Nereids) was born Achilles, the most celebrated hero of the Trojan War, but the semi-divine marriage was itself, in a certain sense, the real prelude to the conflict.
The splendid nuptial banquet on Mount Pelion, during which the Muses sang the epithalamium (the wedding song), was attended by all, and rich were the gifts: among the most precious were an ash-wood spear from the Centaur Chiron, who later became Achilles's mentor, and Poseidon's two immortal horses, Balius and Xanthus, which later played their part in the war by pulling Achilles' chariot. Among the attending gods was Eris (Discord), who at the height of the celebrations threw down a golden apple, declaring that it should be awarded to the fairest of three goddesses: Athena, Hera, and Aphrodite. A dispute immediately broke out, and no one was willing to shoulder the thankless job of choosing among the three. To restore order, Zeus ordered Hermes to lead the three goddesses to Mount Ida, where the Trojan prince Paris would have judged the contest.

THE JUDGEMENT OF PARIS

The arrival of the divine trio frightened the young prince Paris, son of Hecuba and Priam king of Troy, and he attempted to flee. Hermes reassured him that he had nothing to fear and that, quite the contrary, he had been chosen by the Father of the Gods to judge the rival claims of Athena, Aphrodite, and Hera. He therefore listened carefully to the arguments advanced by each goddess and to their promises of extravagant gifts in return for the coveted golden apple. Athena offered wisdom and victory in all combat; Hera, sovereignty over all Asia; Aphrodite, the eternal love of Helen of Sparta, whose beauty was sung throughout the known world. Although all the offers were enticing, with no hesitation Paris decreed Aphrodite the winner.
Helen was the daughter of Zeus and Leda, and therefore the sister of Castor and Pollux (the Dioscuri) and of Clytemnestra, who later played an important role in the war. Dazzled by eastern prince's looks and his extraordinary wealth, she

One of the great 4th century BC bronze statues recently discovered at Piraeus, the port of ancient Athens, has been identified as the young Trojan prince Paris, who was called upon to judge the fairest of the goddesses, as he offers the apple of victory (now lost, but probably made of gold) to Aphrodite. In exchange, the goddess had promised Paris the love of Helen of Sparta, the most beautiful of mortal women, and so set in motion the events that ended in the Trojan War.
Piraeus, Archaeological Museum.

Facing page, the mythical judgement of Paris as imagined by Scarsellino (Ippolito Scarsella, 1550-1620).
Florence, Uffizi.

consented without a second thought to follow her love to his homeland. She took much Spartan treasure and many slaves with her, but abandoned her only daughter, Hermione, the child of her lawful husband Menelaus, king of Sparta and son of Atreus.
But there had been a prologue. When Helen was still very young, the court of her "earthly" father Tyndareus was besieged by numerous suitors, all of whom—before it was even remotely possible to know which would be chosen—pledged to defend her chosen husband against anyone who in the future might have laid claim to her hand.
It was this promise by so many valiant princes that made Helen's crude betrayal of Menelaus a matter of state that led to war, a war in which one of the combatant forces was no less than a true Panhellenic army.

The Greeks' first move was to send an ambassador to Troy to demand the return of Helen to her rightful husband, but when all diplomatic efforts to resolve the matter peacefully proved vain, war became inevitable.

Achilles at Scyros

Heralds were sent throughout Greece to summon volunteers for the expedition to Troy, in Asia. Since an oracle had revealed to Peleus (or in another version of the myth, to Thetis) that their son would die under the walls of Troy, Peleus disguised Achilles as a girl and sent him to the court of King Lycomedes at Scyros, where he lived for nine years among Lycomedes's daughters under the pseudonym Pyrrha ("tawny," from the color of his hair). During his long stay in Scyros, divested of his disguise and calling himself Pyrrhus, Achilles paired with one of the king's daughters, Deidamia; she gave him a son whom she also called Pyrrhus, although he later took the name of Neoptolemus and participated in the long Trojan War after the death of Achilles. The Pelide (son of Peleus) was nevertheless unable to elude his destiny. Odysseus, mindful of the prophecy of the seer Calchas that Troy could not by taken unless the young Achilles joined the expedition, set out in search of him and finally arrived at the court of Lycomedes disguised as a merchant. On the pretext of displaying his goods, he was admitted to the women's apartments; when he spread his precious wares the women of the court were immediately attracted by his materials for embroidery and his fabrics, while "Pyrrha" lighted on some precious weapons cunningly placed by Odysseus among the other goods. His true identity thus revealed, Achilles could no longer remain in hiding; nor could Peleus and Thetis any longer oppose his calling as a warrior.

Above, Achilles' mother Thetis holds shield and spear for her son while he puts on his leg armor. Peleus, his father and the king of Phthia, stands on the left, while Achilles' son Neoptolemus stands on the right. Center tondo of a black-figure plate decorated by the painter Lydos (ca. 550 BC). Athens, National Archaeological Museum.

Facing page, the Centaur Chiron was the young Achilles' patient and devoted tutor. Oil-on-canvas (1782) by J. B. Regnault. Paris, Louvre.

Aeneas, holding a shield bearing a lion, walks in front of Paris as he leads Helen from the kingdom of Sparta. Eros, symbolizing passionate love, and Peithos (persuasion) cover Helen's head as a sign of her infatuation while Aphrodite gives encouragement from behind, accompanied by a young servant. Drawing after a red-figure Attic skyphos made by Hieron and painted by Makron (ca. 490 BC). Boston, Museum of Fine Arts.

A despairing Agamemnon about to sacrifice his daughter Iphigeneia to placate the ire of Artemis. 18th century fresco by G. B. Tiepolo. Vicenza (Italy), Villa Valamarana.

The Departure for Troy and the Sacrifice of Iphigeneia

The troops gathered at Argos in the kingdom of Agamemnon, the commander-in-chief of the Greek forces, and then set sail toward Aulis. When their progress was slow for lack of a wind, the seer Calchas was again consulted; he explained that they were becalmed at the will of Artemis, who had been angered by Agamemnon. Some sources suggest that he had been negligent in her regard in various manners, either by killing a deer, an animal sacred to the goddess, and boasting that Artemis herself could not have done better; or because once Agamemnon's father Atreus had not sacrificed the finest of his flocks, the golden lamb, to Artemis and, as was the rule in antiquity, his guilt had passed to his son; or that Agamemnon was sullied with perjury, having promised to sacrifice the finest newborn creature to Artemis in the year his daughter Iphigeneia had been born, and had not offered her the life of his daughter.
Whatever the cause of Artemis' anger, Calchas revealed that the only way to appease the goddess was to sacrifice Iphigeneia. This time, since Agamemnon was spurred by his own ambition and concern for the public good, but above all because he was urged on by his companions (and especially by Odysseus and Menelaus), it appeared unlikely that his daughter would be saved. At the time, Iphigeneia was in Argos with her mother; Agamemnon sent a message ordering the girl's immediate departure for Aulis, where she was to be married to Achilles before the departure of the fleet. Iphigeneia arrived, obedient to her father's summons, but instead of marrying, she was sacrificed to Artemis at the hand of Calchas. In other versions, the goddess was moved with pity at the last minute, and by substituting a fawn for the maiden saved her and conducted her to Tauris (in today's Crimea), where she became one of her priestesses.

The Iliad *narrates the preludes and the legendary events of the long war that ended with the Athenians' annihilation of Troy, and consequently presents a well-stocked gallery of heroes who owe their lasting fame to this masterpiece of ancient literature. A poem of war and death, of action and hate, the* Iliad *begins with Homer's celebrated invocation to the Muse that she might inspire his song:*
"Sing, O goddess, the anger of Achilles son of Peleus..."

THE WAR

The Siege of Troy

Achilles waits in ambush behind the fountain where Troilus goes to water his horse, in an Etruscan painting (6th cent. BC). Tarquinia, Tomb of the Bulls.

With wind filling their sails at last, the Greek fleet set sail and eventually reached the Troad (Troas, the area around Troy), dropping anchor off the island of Tenedos and establishing their base camp there. The Greeks had been encamped for nine years outside the walls of Troy (in today's Turkey, near the mouth of the Hellespont) before the events related in the *Iliad* began to unfold. Various sources, in most cases postdating the great Homeric poem, relate encounters (or better, skirmishes) that took place during the course of those first nine years, mainly incursions by pirates and episodes of banditry to the detriment of the islands and the nearby cities of Asia Minor. Notable among these chronicles is the capture of Thebe in Mysia by Achilles (where Chryseis was taken in the plunder of the city and later presented to Agamemnon), and the expedition against Lyrnessus, where Achilles took the slave girl Briseis captive.
The most celebrated conflicts involving the direct engagement of the Greek and Trojan armies took place immediately following the Greeks' landing, when victory went to the Trojans. Later, however, after Achilles had killed Cycnus, son of Poseidon, the tide turned against Troy and the Trojans were forced to retreat inside their city walls.

The Ambush of Troilus

Another important event occurred during to the early stages of the war, but it is narrated in detail only by sources later than Homer. We might even say that it was a fundamental episode, since it proved instrumental in determining the final victory of the Greeks. According to the prophecy of a celebrated oracle, Troy could not be captured if Troilus, the youngest son of Priam and Hecuba (or according to another tradition of Apollo and Hecuba), lived to

The Greek camp outside Troy. Detail of a painting by Charles Vernet (1758-1836) of the funeral games held in honor of Patrocles. Mexico City, San Carlos Museum.

the age of twenty. So, shortly after the Greeks encamped outside the city, Achilles slew Troilus after laying in ambush for him near the spring where the young prince would go to water his horses, often in the company of his sister Polyxena who would draw water from the cool spring.

The Wrath of Achilles

The events narrated in the Homeric poem begin in the tenth year of the war and open with the dispute between Achilles and Agamemnon over possession of the slave girl Briseis. The Greek forces were being decimated by a terrible plague and the seer Calchas was summoned once again. He revealed that the scourge was a manifestation of the anger of Apollo and had been inflicted on them through the intervention of the priest Chryses, whose daughter Chryseis had been captured during the battle of Thebes and assigned to Agamemnon as booty. Achilles summoned all the Greek leaders to council, and they handed down an injunction to Agamemnon to restore Chryseis to her father. Agamemnon agreed to bide by the decision on condition that Briseis, the young slave girl kept by Achilles, be given to him in exchange. Achilles withdrew to his tent angered, convinced he was the victim of an injustice and high-handedness, and swore not to take further part in the conflict until his right to keep the girl was acknowledged. When Agamemnon's heralds came to claim Briseis, Achilles did not refuse to let her go but, deeply offended, went to the water's edge and invoked the name of his mother Thetis. Thetis knew full well

Armed and armored soldiers running into battle in a detail from a black-figure Attic vase (6th cent. BC). Naples, National Archaeological Museum.

Agamemnon's envoys take the slave girl Briseis. Detail from a Greek skyphos attributed to the ceramist Hieron and the painter Makron (5th cent. BC). Paris, Louvre.

that the Greeks would not gain victory over the Trojans until Achilles joined in the battle, so she advised her son to allow the Trojans to attack, and even to let them advance as far as the ships; when the situation became untenable it would have been impossible even for the arrogant Agamemnon not to come to terms with Achilles. Furthermore, Thetis interceded for her son with Zeus, who agreed to give the Trojans the upper hand in the conflict for as long as Achilles remained withdrawn from the fighting.

Facing page, Thetis intercedes with Zeus for her son Achilles in a 19th century painting by Jean Auguste Dominique Ingres, who took his inspiration for the figure of the Father of the Gods from the description of the colossal statue of Zeus enthroned sculpted by Phidias in the 5th century BC for the Temple of Olympia. Aix-en-Provence (France), Musée Granet.

When Agamemnon took the slave girl Briseis from Achilles he caused the hero such offence that he refused to take further part in the fighting, and passed the time playing dice with his faithful friend Ajax. Black-figure Attic amphora (ca. 510 BC). Rome, National Museum at Villa Giulia.

The Death of Patrocles

As Thetis had foreseen, when the Trojans had advanced so far as to place the Greeks in grave danger of defeat Agamemnon sent envoys to Achilles imploring him to take up arms again and promising to return Briseis to him. He also offered a munificent reward, twenty of the most beautiful Trojan women, and the hand of one of his daughters. But despite this and the

The funeral games organized by Achilles in honor of his faithful friend Patrocles, killed by Hector, take place before the Greek troops, who pay homage to the valor of the fallen hero. Fragment of a black-figure dinos or lebes (deep wine cup on a low foot) signed by the great Athenian painter Sophilos (ca. 580 BC) and discovered at Pharsalos (Thessaly, Greece). Athens, National Archaeological Museum.

Below, the struggle over the corpse of Achilles' friend Patrocles, killed in battle against the Trojans. Detail of a Classical-era Greek krater, in the style of the master Exekias (ca. 530 BC), from Pharsalos. Athens, National Archaeological Museum.

A lively scene of the chariot race, the star event of the funeral games called in honor of Patrocles. Oil-on-canvas by Charles Vernet. (1758-1836). Mexico City, San Carlos Museum.

warnings of Patrocles, his faithful friend since childhood and his companion on this as on many other expeditions, that the situation was indeed critical, the hero was adamant in his refusal. When Patrocles realized there was no way to change Achilles' mind, he instead changed tack and obtained leave to return to the battlefield himself accompanied by the Myrmidons, Achilles' select body of fighters, and to use Achilles's arms and armor. The sole sight of Patrocles so arrayed convinced the Trojans that the hero was again fighting with the Greeks and struck stark terror into their ranks.
Patrocles and his contingent advanced and were soon dealing death to the Trojans. Just as the enemy forces had turned to retreat, Patrocles reached the chariot of the valorous Hector, the eldest son of Priam king of Troy and leader of the Trojan sortie. Patrocles felled the charioteer Cebriones, but Apollo intervened on Hector's behalf and guided his armed hand to kill Patrocles. The Greeks and Trojans began fighting for possession of Patrocles' body (already stripped of the divine armor given to Achilles by his mother Thetis and originally forged by Hephaestus as a wedding present for his father Peleus). News of Patrocles' death and depredation came to Achilles, who, grief-stricken but furious for revenge, advanced unarmed into the thick of the fray. With a single terrifying cry he put the Trojans to flight, and his friend's body was recovered. In honor of Patrocles, Achilles organized magnificent funeral celebrations, including a solemn sacrifice of twelve young Trojans and the traditional games in which all the Greek leaders participated.

Achilles' Vengeance

Achilles' grief and anger at the death of Patrocles, and his desire for vengeance, drove him back into the conflict. To Agamemnon, he expressed his readiness to fight at his side once more, and he donned the new armor Thetis had had forged for him by Hephaestus. As he returned to battle his horse Xanthus, momentarily and miraculously granted the gifts of prophecy and of speech, announced to its master that his death was imminent.
Careless of this prophecy and disdaining every danger, Achilles threw himself among the Trojans and they fled in terror. Only Aeneas, inspired by Apollo, remained to face the fury of the son of Peleus. But when Achilles pierced Aeneas's shield with his spear and Aeneas was about to counterattack by throwing an enormous rock, Poseidon intervened to separate the combatants and kept them both from harm by engulfing them in a cloud. Aeneas was destined for far greater things than to be slain by Achilles beneath the walls of Troy!
Hector too was eager to fight Achilles, but their destinies kept them apart for the time. Achilles thus continued his advance on Troy, forging the river Scamander and taking many young Trojans prisoner for later sacrifice on the tomb of Patrocles. The river-god attempted to stop the slaughter by attacking Achilles, whose victims were damming his waters: the river rose and flowed out of its bed in pursuit of the hero, but in the end it was forced by Hephaestus to desist and return to its normal course.

Bottom, the triumphant Achilles urges his horses on as he drags Hector's body, tied to his chariot, around the walls of Troy to the horror of the Trojans under siege. Painting by Franz Matsch for Empress Elisabeth of Austria's Achilleion *on Corfu.*

Top, Achilles preparing his horse for battle. Fragment of a black-figure bowl signed by the great Athenian painter Nearchos (ca. 560 BC). Athens, National Archaeological Museum.

The shade of Patrocles appears to the sleeping Achilles in an 18th century painting by Gamelin. Montpellier (France), Musée Fabre.

As Achilles sped on toward the city walls to cut off the retreating Trojans, Apollo again intervened, this time to confuse Achilles and make him lose his way. When Achilles was again free to move to attempt to intercept the retreating Trojan troops, he found he was too late and that they had already entered the city and barred the gates.

Only one Trojan warrior waited outside to confront the Pelide: Hector. Despite the supplications of king Priam, who from the city walls on high called out to his son, pleading and renting his hair, Hector stood his ground. But as Achilles approached and the moment of confrontation drew near, dread overcame even the Trojan prince, who ran. As Achilles pursued him three times around the walls, Zeus balanced the destinies of the two heroes on the divine scales and noticed that the death of Hector had become heavier. From that moment on not even Apollo could have done anything for his favorite and heir of Troy.

What is more, Hector now also had Athena against him: in the likeness of Deiphobus, one of Hector's surviving brothers, she convinced Hector that together they could defeat Achilles, and when Hector realized that he had been deceived he was already falling mortally wounded. But before dying he predicted Achilles's approaching death and requested that his own body be returned to his aged father Priam. The contemptuous Achilles, still irate over the death of Patrocles, ignored Hector's request and horribly mutilated the corpse of his enemy who had taken his beloved Patrocles: after slitting the feet and tying the body to his chariot, he dragged it at length around the walls of Troy before returning with it to his camp. Unsatisfied with the pain and humiliation thus inflicted on the Trojans, and in particular on Hector's parents whose son had represented their last hope of deliverance for themselves and their city, Achilles renewed the offense daily. After twelve days of this, Zeus commanded Thetis to inform Achilles of the extent of the gods' indignation over Achilles' utter lack of respect for a dead foe. Priam thus came to the Achaean camp to ransom his son's body, and when he did Achilles was moved to pity, since the old man and broken king reminded him of his own father whom he would never see again—and he agreed to surrender the mangled body for ceremonial burial.

The Death of Achilles

The death of Hector set in motion the wheels of destiny that were to bring about Achilles' end. As the hero was leaving to go to war, Thetis had warned him of the fate that awaited him: by fighting the Trojan War Achilles would earn immortal glory instead of the dreary destiny reserved him if he stayed at home, but his death on the expedition would be an early one, coming soon after the fall of Hector. There are numerous traditions regarding the death of Achilles: some say he was felled in the thick of the fighting by an arrow shot by Paris but guided by Apollo; others that Paris shot Achilles as the latter was going, unarmed, to a tryst with Polyxena, one of the daughters of Priam and Hecuba. According to one version, Achilles was enamored of Polyxena and requested that she be delivered to him as ransom for the body of Hector; the exchange was to take place in the temple of Apollo Thymbraeus, not far from the gates of Troy. Here, Paris lay in wait for the hero behind the statue of the god and shot Achilles in the heel. As is well known, Thetis was concerned for the possible consequences of the mortality inherited by her sons from their father Peleus and submerged them in the miraculous waters of the Styx, the river of the Underworld, to make them immortal. When it was Achilles' turn, however, his mother held him firmly by the heel, which remained unwetted by the waters. It was only by directing his arrow into the one vulnerable spot on Achilles' body that Paris was able to slay the hero.

The old and infirm Priam implores Achilles to return Hector's corpse. Red-figure skyphos decorated by the Brygos Painter. Vienna, Kunsthistorisches Museum.

Facing page, the dispute over Achilles' weapons reached heights of unheard-of violence, due to the value attributed by all to the trophies. Detail of an Attic lekythos (5th cent. BC). Taranto (Italy), National Archaeological Museum.

The Dispute over the Arms of Achilles and the Suicide of Ajax

Ajax, son of Telamon and king of Salamis, had brought a modest contingent of twelve ships to engage in the expedition against Troy. Tall, strong, and very handsome, he was always calm of demeanor and self-assured; among the Greek heroes, he was second in importance only to Achilles thanks to his courage and skill in battle. And so, when after the death of Achilles Thetis announced that his armor would go to the most valorous of the Greeks, or at least to the hero who most inspired terror in the ranks of the Trojans, Ajax was convinced that it would be his. But when the Trojan prisoners were asked who they most feared, out of spite they named Odysseus and not Ajax; denied what he considered his rightful prize, Ajax took offence. That night his mood turned to madness and he slaughtered much of the livestock kept to victual the Greek troops, believing the animals to be the Achaean leaders. In the morning, when he recovered his senses and realized what he had done, he was so shamed by his the taint of his guilt that he committed suicide by throwing himself on his own sword.

Facing page, the tragic drama of Ajax as interpreted in a 19th century painting by Francesco Sabatelli. Florence, Palazzo Pitti, Gallery of Modern Art.

A small Etruscan bronze of Ajax's suicide, found at Populonia (Italy).

Ajax places his sword in the ground in preparation for his suicide after Agamemnon refused to grant him the arms of Achilles after the death of the hero in battle. Drawing after a black-figure amphora by the great Athenian painter Exekias (ca. 540 BC). Museum of Boulogne-sur-Seine (France).

Cassandra, Laocoon, and the Trojan Horse

After ten years of war during which victory appeared certain first for one side and then for the other, the Greeks no longer knew what strategy to adopt to secure victory and finally return home. But the brilliant and cunning Odysseus, king of Ithaca, came to their aid: he had for some time been entertaining the idea of entering the city by stealth and attacking from within with warriors hidden inside a huge wooden horse. By his plan, the Trojans themselves would have dragged the horse into Troy, believing it an offering to Athena, and then the Greeks would have cut them down in their sleep; to make the story of the horse more plausible, the Greek Sinon, pretending to be a traitor, would have recounted how the Achaeans had deserted and burnt their camp and withdrawn to their ships (which, as they were anchored behind the island of Tenedos, happened not to be visible from Troy).
Thus it was, and when the Trojans saw the horse and Sinon had explained that it had been left by the Greeks as a propitiatory offering to the goddess Athena to speed them on their journey home, and that it had been built so large to prevent the Trojans from dragging it into their city to themselves offer it to the goddess, they rejoiced and gave thanks in the belief that they had seen the last of their dreaded enemies. They also set about inventing a way to

Facing page, Laocoon and his sons are crushed by serpents sent by Apollo. The priest had warned the Trojans against introducing the wooden horse into the city. Monumental sculptural group by and Athanadoros, Hagesandros, and Polydoros of Rhodes (ca. 50 BC), a copy of a bronze original dated to 140-139 BC. Rome, Vatican Museums.

The fallen Troy invaded by the Greek troops, in a Mannerist painting (early 17th cent.). Blois (France), Fine Arts Museum.

In the dead of night, fully-armed Greek soldiers emerge from the wooden horse (on wheels for better mobility!). Odysseus' cunning plan permitted the Greeks to enter Troy after a ten-year siege and proceed to sack and destroy the city. Drawing after the decoration on the neck of a pithos (large earthenware jar) with other decoration in relief, produced in the Cyclades, probably on the island of Tinos (ca. 670 BC). Mykonos, Archaeological Museum.

conduct the wonderful horse into the city, even going so far as to demolish one of the gates of their stronghold. But not all Trojans joined in the celebrations in the streets of Troy, or trusted in the good faith of the Greeks in general and of Sinon in particular. The most vehemently opposed to bringing the horse into Troy were Cassandra, one of the daughters of Priam and Hecuba, and Laocoon, the priest of Apollo. While the horse still stood on the beach, Laocoon took a spear from one of the warriors and hurled it against the body of the mighty horse *cum* siege tower. The impact produced a hollow sound, but none of the Trojans believed him when he explained that the horse was sure to be some treacherous invention of the crafty Odysseus.

Nor was the young Cassandra believed. She had been granted the gift of prophecy by Apollo, who had taught her the art of future-gazing in return (he hoped) for her favors, but Cassandra refused to keep her part of the bargain and therefore incurred Apollo's anger. Apollo did not deprive her of her prophetic gift, but by spitting in her mouth doomed her to never being believed. And thus, even though

Greek warriors. Detail of an Attic red-figure vase (5th cent. BC). Naples, National Archaeological Museum.

The Trojan War. Ajax tears Cassandra from the foot of the statue of Athena. Illustration by Alexandre de La Borde (1813) after a Greek vase. Paris, Decorative Arts Library.

she revealed the truth about the horse, she was ignored just as she had been on other important occasions before and during the extenuating war: when her brother Paris returned disguised to the city after carrying off Helen, Cassandra prophesied that he would bring about the downfall of his people; when he later reappeared accompanied by Helen, Cassandra announced that the abduction of the wife of Menelaus would be the cause of the destruction of their city.

Laocoon's fate was even more cruel. As he hurried to the water's edge to offer a bull in sacrifice to Poseidon in order to bring down a storm on the Greek fleet, two monstrous sea serpents emerged from the water and attacked his two sons, wrapping them in their terrible coils; while trying to free them he too was caught in their fatal coils; all three were crushed to death and devoured by the monsters. The Trojans interpreted this event as Laocoon's punishment for the lack of respect shown the goddess Athena when he had hurled the spear against the horse. Instead, although it was in fact a punishment, it was sent by Apollo, who was angry with the priest for once having profaned his temple by making love to his wife behind the statue of the god. The Trojans knew nothing of this, however, and so the fateful horse was made to enter the city.

The Destruction of Troy

The day of the Greeks' feigned departure was a day of jubilation for the Trojans, who sang, danced, and drank wine all day and far into the night. Sinon was thus able to act undisturbed, and when he saw that all the city was asleep he climbed onto the ramparts and waved a torch to signal to the ships anchored off Tenedos that all had proceeded according to plan. He then returned to the wooden horse and released from its girth the warriors hidden within; they immediately spread out through the city, killing and burning as they went. The Trojans, surprised in their sleep and in the main still suffering the aftereffects of their heady celebrations, fought back as best they could, hurling tableware, spits, and even the flaming beams and rafters of their own homes against the enemy. But this time nothing could stop the fury of the Greeks, utterly exacerbated by ten long years of war. Some of their actions were exceptionally cruel: Neoptolemus, the young son of Achilles, mercilessly slaughtered the aged king Priam who had taken shelter near the altar of Zeus; Hector's son Astyanax was wrenched with unheard-of violence from the arms of his mother Andromache and flung over the city walls to his death by a detail of Greek soldiers; Ajax son of Oileus (the "Lesser Ajax") threw himself on Cassandra, who had taken refuge in the temple of Athena where she was priestess, and ignominiously tore her garments. There was nothing now that even the great Athena could do to help her worshipers: the fate of Troy was sealed and destiny ran its course. When it became clear that all was lost, the courageous Aeneas, who had fought heroically until the very last, abandoned the battle. Carrying his aged father Anchises on his shoulders, he led his wife Creusa and his son Ascanius from the city. He was protected in his escape by his mother Aphrodite, and as he fled he took with him the city's tutelary gods, the Penates. As Aphrodite explained to Aeneas, it was not his destiny to die at Troy, but rather to live to found a city in the West, a city which, "risen from the ashes of Troy," would one day rule over the entire world.

Top, Menelaus and Elena on the body of a Greek amphora produced at Pamphaios; on the neck, a Nereid with two fish (ca. 530-510 BC). Paris, Louvre.

Center, Clytemnestra killing Cassandra, who vainly seeks refuge at an altar. Tondo inside a red-figure Attic cup (ca. 430 BC). Ferrara (Italy), National Archaeological Museum.

Bottom, Clytemnestra and her lover Aegisthus kill Agamemnon on his return from Troy (ca. 630 BC). Earthenware votive tablet from Gortyn in Crete. Herakleion, Archaeological Museum.

The gold leaf funeral mask known as the Mask of Agamemnon discovered by Heinrich Schliemann in a tomb in the First Circle of tombs at Mycenae. Athens, National Archaeological Museum.

Homeward Bound

The events that followed the war proper were narrated in the *Odyssey* and in other later poems of the epic cycle known as the *Nostoi* ("returns"). The later life of Menelaus was relatively serene: despite everything, he was eventually reconciled with Helen, whom he had always loved, and after a journey lasting eight years returned home accompanied by his legitimate consort.
The events surrounding Menelaus' brother Agamemnon and his family were much more complex and tragic, and in any case the direct consequence of the deeds of the Greek leader during the Trojan War. Clytemnestra remained faithful to Agamemnon until she heard of his possession of the slave-girl Chryseis. At that time Clytemnestra was being courted by the insistent young Aegisthus, whom she resisted until he banished her faithful counselor, the *aedo* Demodocus, from court. She thus heard of Agamemnon's unfaithfulness and finally gave in to Aegisthus, who ruled as king in the riverside palace in Argos until the return of Agamemnon. Aegisthus himself ordered sentinels posted along the shore to signal by torch the return of the royal ship.

A sumptuous banquet was prepared for the king's homecoming; during the celebrations Aegisthus, with some twenty accomplices concealed in the hall, murdered Agamemnon in front of Clytemnestra. Another version of the myth has it that Clytemnestra herself stabbed her husband after his bath: she had given him a robe with the openings sewn up, and while he was struggling to dress she was able to stab him with no fear of resistance. She thus would have avenged the death of Iphigeneia, sacrificed by her father to Artemis in order to secure a favorable wind for the departure of the Greek fleet from Aulis.
Another victim of implacable Fate was Cassandra, whose unhappy life was ended by a blow from an axe wielded by Clytemnestra, who held her guilty of having become, willingly or not, Agamemnon's favorite concubine after she was allotted to him as part of the booty taken from Troy.
And yet, the bloody history begun with the sacrifice of Iphigeneia did not end until many years later when Orestes, son of Agamemnon and Clytemnestra, returned home from the involuntary exile into which he had been sent as a child by his preceptor to subtract him from Clytemnestra's vindictive fury. Upon his return to Argos, Orestes put both his mother and her lover to death.

Chasing a Dream: The Gold of Troy

300 - 600 AD
Decline and final abandonment of the city

300 BC - 300 AD
Troy IX, the Hellenistic and later Roman Ilium

700-300 BC
Troy VIII, the Classical Ilium

1000-700 BC
Site abandoned

1250 - 1000 BC
Troy VII

1800 - 1250 BC
Troy VI, the Homeric city (?)

1900 - 1800 BC
Troy V

2000-1900 BC
Troy IV

2200-2000 BC
Troy III

2500-2200 BC
Troy II, the citadel of "Priam's Treasure"

3600-2500 BC
Troy I

3600 BC
Foundation of Troy

The last of the heroes that made Troy immortal was not sung by Homer—but from Homer he gleaned the basic information he needed to make his dream of a lifetime come true. Driven by his enthusiastic and passionate character, his love for scholarship, and his undisputed capabilities (among other things, he taught himself between 8 and 13 languages including modern and ancient Greek), Heinrich Schliemann, born in 1822 in the out-of-the-way village of Neubukow in Mecklenburg-Schwerin, became a unique figure in modern archaeology. This courageous and independent spirit worked at many trades before founding a business of his own; he traveled worldwide and created a true economic empire. His success was such as to provide the bases for a landmark decision: to dedicate all his energies and resources to an impossible dream he had been caressing since he was eight years old—to find Troy.

His only point of reference: his beloved Homeric epics, despite the skepticism of the "experts" who considered them works of pure fantasy. Encouraged by the shared enthusiasm of his second wife the Greek schoolgirl Sophia Engastromenos, in 1870 Schliemann began excavating the mound at Hisarlik, in Turkey—and in just a few years succeeded in transforming legend into history. Believing that Homeric Troy must be at the lowest level, he brought to light nine strata dated from 3600 BC to 1500 AD, nine phases in the life of a great settlement that had "always" dominated the Dardanelles: Troy.
And as the mythical city was uncovered so were its fabulous treasures—bracelets, diadems, necklaces, and exquisitely made jewelry of all kinds. Even though the trove (which Schliemann smuggled out of Turkey) was far down and predated the Homeric king by centuries, it was immediately baptized "Priam's Treasure."
Later in life Schliemann also excavated Mycenae and Tiryns, but his name will forever be linked to his first, incomparable love: the city of Priam and Aeneas.

A portrait of Heinrich Schliemann as an older man.
Below and facing page, the discovery of the majestic remains of the mythical city of Troy in period images.

Sophia Schliemann in 1875, wearing splendid jewelry from the fabulous "Treasure" believed to be Priam's.

CHAPTER V

THE ODYSSEY: THE WANDERINGS OF ODYSSEUS

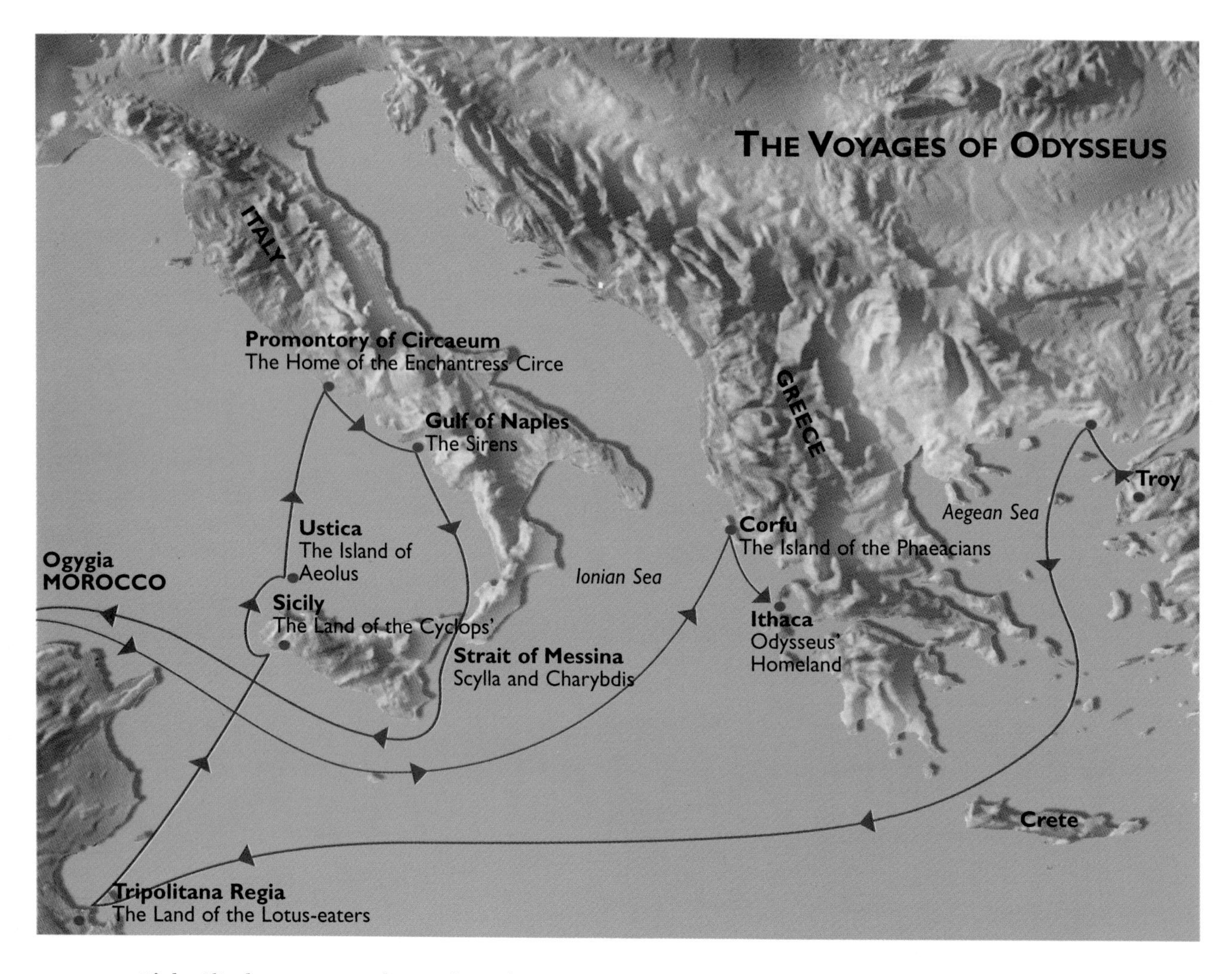

If the Iliad is a poem of war, the Odyssey *is the poem of adventure, daring, and faithfulness. In counterpoint to the "godlike Achilles" stands the "ingenious hero" Odysseus, astute and fearless and at the same time extraordinarily human. Co-protagonist of the poem, with Odysseus, is the sea, the element the hero and his companions cross on their dangerous and to some fatal voyage, the element in which Odysseus must trust if he is ever to return home.*

The Lotus-eaters

After a stormy departure from Troy caused by a quarrel with Menelaus, reunion with Agamemnon's contingent, and finally separation from it during a severe storm, Odysseus sailed south until a strong north wind drove him to Kythera and, two days later, to the land of the Lotus-eaters, which is usually identified with Tripolitana in the area of today's Lybia. A few of the men, sent ahead by Odysseus to explore the land, were given a warm welcome by the inhabitants and offered the delicious fruit of the lotus on which they lived. At the taste of the fruit, Odysseus' companions lost all memory of their homeland and any desire to leave Lotus-land. It was only by force that Odysseus was able to drag the men back to the ships and set sail again.

Polyphemus and the Land of the Cyclops

Now sailing northward, the heroes came to an island with many goats with which they thought to provision the ships before departing again. They had come to the land of the Cyclops', unanimously identified with Sicily.
The Cyclops' were monstrous giants of extraordinary strength but with only one eye. Their only wealth was their flocks, which they guarded assiduously, and, although many myths speak of their participation in the fortification of various cities, they were actually unable to build and equally unable to living in a sociable manner. They thus lived, each with his sheep, in inhospitable caves; and although they had fire they did not use it and ate raw, animal and human, flesh. When Odysseus and his men came into their land, they entered the cave of Polyphemus, the leader of the Cyclops', who was momentarily absent. Odysseus' companions urged taking as many sheep and cheeses as they could carry and leaving quickly. Odysseus refused to steal, but when Polyphemus returned and discovered the men in his cavern he began devouring them two at a time. Odysseus then offered him some wine, which the Cyclops was not used to drinking, and he soon became more benevolent toward the intruders. When the Cyclops asked Odysseus his name, the hero once again demonstrated his shrewdness, answering "Oudeis" ("nobody" in Greek and easily confused with "Odysseus"). Polyphemus, by this time in his cups, cheerily promised that he would eat Odysseus last, in thanks for the wine; he then drank another bowl of it—and fell into a deep sleep. Odysseus and his remaining companions took advantage of the situation immediately: they hardened a wooden stake on the fire and thrust it into the Cyclops' eye, blinding him. Even so, Polyphemus sought

The blinding of the Cyclops Polyphemus by Odysseus and his companions is a favorite subject on Etruscan vases, like this one (530 BC). Rome, National Museum at Villa Giulia.

On the following pages, a dramatic depiction of Odysseus blinding Polyphemus, by Pellegrino Tibaldi (1527-96). Bologna (Italy), Palazzo Poggi.

to prevent their escape in the morning by blocking the opening of the cave, but Odysseus had foreseen this too and had come up with an ingenious system for saving himself and his men: they hung under the sheep's bellies to escape Polyphemus' searching hands as he counted the beasts as they filed out to pasture. And when Polyphemus, crying out from the pain of his wound and furious at having been tricked, called on the other Cyclops' for help, they thought him mad and would not listen. Things only

worsened when they asked him who had set on him: poor Polyphemus could only answer with a resigned "Oudeis"—"Nobody." When the heroes were safe and sound on their ship and pulling out to sea, Ulysses called out his true name: Polyphemus realized that an ancient oracle predicting that he would be blinded by "Odysseus" had been fulfilled. Following this episode, Polyphemus' father Poseidon did everything in his power to prevent Odysseus from returning home.

The Island of Aeolus

The surviving company then sailed on until they reached the island of Aeolus, the god of the winds, who welcomed them hospitably and gave Odysseus a leather bag containing all the winds save the one most favorable to their navigation, which thus would continue to blow and push the ship straight to Ithaca. Believing the bag contained gold, the sailors opened it one night: all the captive winds escaped and caused a raging storm. The company was thus literally thrown in the opposite direction and only after the tempest had subsided were they able to land again on the island of Aeolus. Odysseus once again asked Aeolus for a favorable wind, but he was forced to refuse, as it seemed to him quite evident that through the occurrence the gods had manifested their hostility toward Odysseus' return to Ithaca.

Facing page, Polyphemus' fury after being blinded, with Odysseus' escaping companions in the foreground, in a 16th century painting by Pellegrino Tibaldi. Bologna (Italy), Palazzo Poggi.

This page, Aeolus, the mythical and much-feared god of the winds, was capable of unleashing storms but also favorable winds for voyagers. Illuminated capital from a codex decorated by Liberale da Verona (ca. 1445 - ca. 1526). Siena, Cathedral, Piccolomini Library.

Circe's Enchantments

Odysseus continued onward, but by now with little control over his direction since the gods were set against him. After a short stop in the land of the Laestrygonians, cannibals who by tradition lived somewhere on the coast of Italy between Formia and Gaeta, the heroes came to the island of Aeaea, usually identified with the promontory of Circaeum in Latium between Gaeta and Terracina and home of the enchantress Circe. By now an expert in landing on unknown shores, Odysseus sent only a small contingent out to explore the land, and stayed on board ship with most of his men. The avant-garde discovered a splendid palace—and Circe, who invited them to partake of a sumptuous banquet. But the men had barely tasted the delicious food set out for them when Circe used her magical powers to transform them into pigs, dogs, and lions, each according to his temperament and so giving concrete form to the deepest-rooted character traits of each. Luckily, not all of the explorers had entered the palace: the wise Eurylochus had held back, and when he saw what was served for "dessert" he hurried back to the ship to inform Odysseus. The hero courageously decided to visit Circe and attempt to save his companions. As he was crossing the woods that separated the beach from the palace he encountered Hermes, who explained how to render Circe's spell powerless by mixing a magical herb called moly into the food, and further: when he unsheathed his sword the enchantress would swear to anything Odysseus ordered. Hermes gave him a moly plant and sent him on his way; when the hero arrived at the palace, Circe cordially invited him to dine. Before drinking from his cup, Odysseus mixed a little moly with the wine so that when Circe attempted to transform him into one of her animals the spell failed. Odysseus then drew his sword and threatened the witch with death. After she had sworn by the Styx not to harm anyone and to restore Odysseus' men to their original forms, Odysseus spared her life.

Two of Odysseus' companions transformed into pigs by the enchantress Circe in her cave. Red-figure lekythos by an Attic painter (ca. 470 BC). Athens, National Archaeological Museum.

But that was not all: he stayed a month (or, according to another version, a year) enjoying the delights of her table and her person; some accounts say that during hero's and his companions' prolonged sojourn on the island of Aeaea Circe even bore him children. It was during this period that on the advice of Circe Odysseus made a journey to Hades, the land of the dead souls, to consult the spirit of the seer Teiresias who predicted that Odysseus would return home alone, on a foreign ship, and that when he finally reached his palace he would have to avenge himself of a host of suitors for his wife's hand. After this informative side trip, Odysseus took to the sea again; his lover gave him further invaluable advice to aid him in his coming trials.

Left, Odysseus holding Circe at swordpoint to force her to restore his men, whom she had transformed into animals. Relief from the end of a stone Etruscan sarcophagus (4th cent. BC). Orvieto (Italy), Claudio Faina Museum.

An original early 16th century interpretation of Circe by Dosso Dossi (Giovanni Luteri). The enchantress is depicted in a tranquil woodland, surrounded by animals and birds: Odysseus' men transformed into a multifaceted bestiary. Washington, National Gallery of Art.

The Spell of the Sirens

Leaving the promontory of Circaeum behind him and sailing south, Odysseus crossed the Gulf of Naples, on an island near which there lived the Sirens, dangerous sea-monsters, represented in art as terrible birds with the heads of women, daughters of the river-god Achelous and the Muse Melpomene, or of Achelous and Sterope, daughter of the king of Calydon in Aetolia (north of Corinth). With the power of their song they lured sailors close to the rocky coast, where their ships were dashed against the cliffs. The Sirens then picked up the pieces, devouring the unlucky sailors. But Odysseus had been warned of the Sirens by Circe and, astute as always, took all due precautions in order to hear their song and yet escape unscathed: he ordered his sailors to plug their ears with wax after having bound him to the mast of the ship, and further enjoined them not to free him no matter what he might say until the danger well abaft. As the first notes reached his ears Odysseus was overcome with desire to sail straight toward them, but his hardy sailors ignored all his supplications and threats. According to later legend the Sirens threw themselves into the sea from vexation at Odysseus' escape, and drowned.

Top, an Etruscan statuette of a young man with the body of a fish. Perugia (Italy), Archaeological Museum.

Bottom, tied to the mast of his ship, Odysseus listens to the magical song of the Sirens. Roman mosaic from Dougga (Tunisia) (3rd cent. AD). Tunis, Musée du Bardo.

Glaucus and Scylla, two mythical characters whose stories entwine with the fascinating, dangerous sea, as portrayed by Santi di Tito (1536-1603). Sansepolcro (Italy), City Art Gallery.

Scylla and Charybdis

Continuing on his voyage south Odysseus and his crew next encountered the perilous Scylla and Charybdis in the Strait of Messina. These sea-monsters were both originally young women, transformed the one because she has incurred the wrath of Circe, the other the vengeance of the gods. Scylla, who lived on the mainland side of the strait, was punished for having vied with Circe for the love of Glaucus (which, incidentally, was returned). In revenge, Circe mixed magical herbs with the waters of the spring where Scylla usually bathed; thus, as she emerged from the pool, six horrible dogs grew from the lower half of her body while her upper half remained intact. Horrified, Scylla withdrew to a grotto on the water where she hid herself from view but could do nothing to restrain the fierce dogs that were part of her body from attacking and devouring unsuspecting seafarers who ventured too close to her cave. The Sicilian side of the Strait instead hosted the grotto of Charybdis. In her human form this daughter of Gaia and Poseidon had been so insatiably voracious that when Heracles, in one version of the myth, passed her way with the cattle of Geryon she stole and devoured them all. The irate Zeus struck her with lightning and she fell into the sea, where she was transformed into a monster. Ever since, three times a day she sucked in vast quantities of sea water together with everything floating on it, including passing ships, and spewed it out again while she fed on the luckless creatures that had been caught in the whirlpool of her making. In this case as well, Odysseus had been advised by Circe of how to avoid the danger—or at least cut his losses. Circe had explained to him that nobody, not even a god, could escape the power of Charybdis' whirling waters, but that if he steered as close as possible to the opposite coast, where Scylla lay, he would in any case reach Thrinacia, or Sicily, since while Charybdis would have annihilated the ship and all on it in a single gulp, Scylla's dogs would be sated with only six victims; with the monster intent on its meal, the ship could run up full sail and exploit the favorable winds to fly to safety on the Sicilian coast. Odysseus followed Circe's advice, albeit with a heavy heart, and succeeded in saving most of his crew.

The Cattle of the Sun

Having safely reached the shores of Sicily, where Helios (the Sun) pastured his herds of cattle, the heroes were becalmed and could not proceed on their way; and their provisions were running low. Although Odysseus had forbidden his sailors to even venture close to the Sun's fine white cattle, the hungry men disobeyed the order, slaughtered some of the cattle, and feasted on them—and inevitably incurred the Sun's wrath. The god complained to Zeus, who as punishment unleashed a tremendous storm when the heroes took to sea again. The ship was hit by Zeus' lightning and sank; all the sailors drowned. Only Odysseus, who had had no part in the sacrilege, survived clinging to the broken main-mast. He drifted with the current toward Charybdis, where he miraculously avoided being sucked into the whirlpool, and after having been tossed about by the sea for nine days was finally washed up on the island of Calypso.

For the Love of Calypso

Calypso, ("she who lies concealed") was a Nymph of extraordinary beauty, the daughter of Helios (or according to other sources, of Atlas), who lived on the island of Ogygia, generally identified with Ceuta on the Moroccan coast near the Strait of Gibralter. She led a quiet and peaceful life in the midst of her attendants, Nymphs like herself, spinning and weaving, lulled by the singing of her companions. When Odysseus was washed onto her shore she treated him with great generosity, and fell in love with him. Odysseus spent many happy years with her but never forgot Ithaca and in his innermost of hearts longed to return home. When it became clear to Odysseus that Calypso had no intention of ever letting him depart, he prayed to Athena to intercede for him with the Father of the Gods. Zeus sent his messenger Hermes to Calypso, instructing her to cease her amorous ensorcelments and leave Odysseus to his fate. Sadly, she supplied him with the wood necessary to build a raft, with victuals, and with advice on how to navigate by the stars—and then bade farewell to the man she loved so dearly and to whom she had given a son.

A fantastic, phantasmagorical cavern is the secluded backdrop for Odysseus and Calypso in this depiction of their love affair by Jan Breughel the Elder (1568-1625).

Odysseus at the court of Alcinous, king of the Phaeacians, in a 19th century painting by Francesco Hayez. Milan, Palazzo Reale.

The Island of the Phaeacians

No sooner was Odysseus at sea again, and sailing east, than another tempest came upon him; he saved himself by clinging to a piece of the wreckage and then swimming until he eventually reached safety, exhausted and naked, on the shore of the island of the Phaeacians, called Scheria in the *Odyssey* and usually identified with Corcyra (now Corfu). Here, his resources completely spent, he fell asleep in a wood bounded by a river. He was awakened by the shouts and laughter of a group of young women, one of whom was Nausicaa, the lovely daughter of Alcinous, king of the Phaeacians. Their meeting had in fact been planned by Athena, so that Nausicaa might intercede for the hero at the court of her father: the goddess had sent her a dream in which her companions reproved her for her negligence and told her to go in all haste to the river to see to washing the clothes of her whole family. Odysseus covered his nakedness with branches and made his presence known to the group. The young women took fright and ran away—all except Nausicaa, who stood her ground before the hero and even scolded her companions for having failed to observe the sacred rules that imposed offering hospitality to one so obviously sent them by the gods. Odysseus then spoke to her with sweet words, saying that her loveliness had led him to mistake her for a goddess or a Nymph—and with that, her aid was secured. That evening, Nausicaa returned to the city with her companions, but not before having pointed out to Odysseus the way to the palace.

Odysseus was welcomed warmly, to the point that during the sumptuous banquet prepared in his honor, as he recounted his adventures to the delight of all present, he was even offered the hand of Nausicaa, who in truth was quite overcome by the aspect of the splendid hero. Although he was obliged to refuse her hand, having a wife in Ithaca, the Phaeacians were so impressed by the adventures and the dangers the noble mariner had faced during his journey that they were willing to help him nonetheless. They provided him with a ship, and the Phaeacian crew left him in a secluded spot on the island of Ithaca after a short voyage. The Phaeacians, however, suffered the revenge of Poseidon, who wrecked the ship that had carried Odysseus and surrounded their island with massive mountains so that this people of traders and seafarers could no longer use their port, the source of their well-being.

hospitality. When she had run out of excuses for rejecting their advances she invented the famous ruse of weaving the tapestry, or shroud for Laertes, telling the suitors she could not remarry until she had finished it. And so for three years she unraveled her day's weaving every night, to gain time in the hope that Odysseus, to whom she had always remained faithful, would return and put an end to her difficulties.

Meanwhile, Back in Ithaca . . .

While Odysseus was fighting the Trojan War and then attempting to return home, there occurred events in Ithaca that were anything but marginal to the story. When he departed for the war, Odysseus had entrusted the care of his home and his wife to his old friend Mentor, whose faithfulness was so well proven that even Athena sometimes appeared in his guise, as when she accompanied Telemachus on his search for his father or, later, when she aided Odysseus in dispatching the suitors. Penelope, however, was the sole trustee of her husband's property. Odysseus's mother Anticleia died of sorrow shortly after his departure, knowing her son to be far away and exposed to the dangers of war, and his father Laertes withdrew to a life in the country. Penelope became the focus of insistent demands for remarriage: all the young men from the surrounding area, from Dulichium, Same, Zacynthus, and from Ithaca itself (that is, from all the cities over which Odysseus ruled), were eager to gain control over the kingdom's possessions and treasure and sought her hand. These young men were known as the "suitors." Irritated by the queen's continued and adamant rejection, they eventually established themselves in the palace, acting as lords and wasting away Odysseus's wealth in continuous feasting and revels, all the while hoping to bring pressure on Penelope to decide among them. Penelope scolded them severely, but to no avail; on the other hand, she was obliged to tolerate their presence in obedience to the sacred laws of

The tireless Penelope weaves the shroud for her father-in-law Laertes but undoes by night all she has woven by day, and so manages to postpone choosing among the suitors a husband who would succeed Odysseus as king. Her son Telemachus is depicted beside her. Scene on a red-figure Attic skyphos from Chiusi, by the artist known as the Penelope Painter (ca. 440 BC). Chiusi (Italy), National Archaeological Museum.

Odysseus, alone of all the company assembled at the palace, was able to draw the bow in the contest proposed by Penelope. After winning, he eliminated the suitors and regained the throne of Ithaca. Drawing after a red-figure Attic skyphos from Tarquinia, decorated by the Penelope Painter (ca. 440 BC). Berlin, Staatliche Museen.

Right, the patient Penelope in a thoughtful pose as she awaits the return of her husband. Roman statue, copy of a Greek original. Rome, Vatican Museums.

The Homecoming to Ithaca

Odysseus was well aware that time and trial (ten tears at war and ten on the journey home) had so transformed his appearance as to make him virtually unrecognizable to his subjects and countrymen, and, shrewd as ever, decided to keep his identity secret for awhile. But first he made himself known to his trusted swineherd Eumaeus; with Eumaeus' help he met privately with his son Telemachus, grown to manhood since Odysseus' departure. Telemachus took Odysseus, disguised as a beggar, to the palace.

No one recognized the hero except his dog Argus and his old nurse Eurycleia. The old dog rose at the sight of his master, wagging his tail—but his ancient heart failed in his joy and he died at Odysseus's feet. Eurycleia did not know the "beggar" immediately, but when she washed his feet in the traditional welcome to guests she recognized a scar from a wound suffered by her master when he was a young man. Odysseus bade her keep his secret, and Eurycleia obeyed.

Meanwhile, Telemachus had been busy: on his father's orders, he put all the suitors' weapons under lock and key. Odysseus then appeared at court before the suitors, asking for something to eat. The

CHAPTER VI

AENEAS: FROM TROY TO ROME

The Aeneid *is the great poem in which Virgil celebrated the heroic epos of Aeneas, who after fleeing Troy—and a long voyage fraught with a thousand perils—landed on the coast of Latium in Italy, where to his descendants Fate had assigned the task of founding Rome. The conception and structure of the epic celebration clearly reflect the* Odyssey *in the passionate account of long years of wandering and later the* Iliad *(or a darkened mirror image of Odysseus' difficult victory over the suitors) in the fierce struggle against the peoples of Latium. And rising above all is the figure of a courageous, pious hero, a worthy progenitor for an Eternal City.*

A Hero of Divine Origin

Aeneas was the son of Anchises, the Trojan prince descended from Dardanus and thereby from Zeus, and of the goddess Aphrodite, who had fallen in love with the mortal Anchises while he was tending father's herds in the mountains of the Troad. The brave warrior Aeneas, who in the Trojan army was considered second in valor only to Hector, had several exchanges with the Greeks under the walls of Troy. He fought with Achilles, but was forced to retreat before his opponent's superior strength; he engaged Diomedes and was wounded by him, but Aphrodite intervened; in her attempt to save her son she was herself wounded, so the battle continued until Apollo dragged Aeneas to safety in a cloud. He was later saved again by the same stratagem, when Poseidon rescued him during another exchange with Achilles after the death of Patrocles and after Aeneas had killed a great number of Greek warriors.

In the Homeric poems, therefore, Aeneas was a hero who enjoyed special protection from the gods, whom he obeyed with respect and devotion. That he was destined for future greatness is equally patent. In Aeneas were in fact vested all the future hopes of the royal house of Troy, above all following the prophecy uttered by Aphrodite when she revealed her true identity to Anchises, who had loved her believing her to be a mere mortal. Aphrodite in fact predicted that their union would bring forth a son thanks to whom the Trojan line would endure for countless centuries.

All these elements were later incorporated and repeated by Virgil in his epic *Aeneid*, and interpreted by the great Latin poet to fit the complex legend that made Rome the heir of the powerful Trojan dynasty and the perpetuator of its historic grandeur.

This page, the expressive and elegant bust of Publius Vergilius Maro (Virgil), the famous Roman poet of Mantuan origin who owes his lasting fame to the composition of the Aeneid.

Facing page, Aeneas flees burning Troy with his father Anchises on his shoulders and his young son Ascanius and his wife Creusa at his side. Although she had been warned not to do so, Creusa turns for a last glimpse of the city in flames in the fresco by Raphael and his assistants known as The Fire in the Borgo *(1515-1517).* Rome, Vatican City, Raphael Rooms.

The Flight from Troy

While the fires set by the Greeks were still burning in Troy, expunged thanks to the treacherously deceptive wooden horse, Aeneas fled the city with his aged father Anchises on his shoulders and with his wife Creusa—who, however, glanced back at the ruined city despite warnings to the contrary and was transformed into a statue of salt—and their young son Ascanius. In his arms, Aeneas cradled the images of the gods most sacred to Troy, the Penates, and a statue of the goddess Pallas Athena known as the Palladium. When he reached nearby Mount Ida (homonymic with a mountain on Crete) he founded a city, but not long afterward he sailed with a fleet of twenty ships to Delos to consult the oracle of Apollo about his own and his compatriots' future.
Told to search out his family's country of origin, he decided to sail on to Crete, the island from which Teucer, one of the earliest of the Trojan kings, had come to Troy. During the night, however, the Penates, the protectors of Trojan families, appeared to him and instructed him to travel on to Italy, the true ancient homeland of his forebears.

Top, a vase painting of Aeneas carrying his weak and aged father Anchises on his back as he leads his young son Ascanius from the burning city of Troy on the night the Greeks finally breached the city walls. Aeneas' flight from the ashes of Priam's glorious city permitted the rise of an illustrious family whose descendent Romulus founded Rome. Drawing after a black-figure Attic amphora (ca. 510 BC). Wurzburg (Germany), Martin von Wagner University Museum.
Bottom, a 16th century painting of the same subject by Federico Barocci. Rome, Borghese Gallery.

Aeneas, aided by his companions, repulses the attack of the terrible Harpies in a painting by François Perrier (1590-1650). Paris, Louvre.

Bottom, the Harpies, monstrous bird-women, tormented Phineus king of Thrace by fouling his table every time he prepared to dine. They were chased away by Calais and Zetes, the winged sons of Boreas, the north wind. As they flew over the seas the Harpies also attacked Aeneas as he journeyed toward Italy. Drawing after the black-figure inside border of a cup by the so-called Painter of Phineus (ca. 530 BC), who worked in the Greek town of Rhegium (now Reggio Calabria, Italy).

On the following pages, Aeneas recounts the fate of the city of Troy to Dido. Sketch by Pierre Guerin for an 1815 oil-on-canvas. Paris, Louvre.

The Journey West

Aeneas thus shifted his sails and set out again, this time in the direction of Hesperia, the Western Mediterranean, and many perilous adventures awaited him along the way. First of all, a violent storm drove him to the Strophades islands, where he and his crew encountered the ferocious Harpies, half woman and half bird; he was blown to Epirus, where he met Helenus, son of Priam king of Troy and husband to Hector's widow Andromache; when he reached the Ionian Sea he landed at various places in southern Italy and visited the many Greek colonies that had been established there; he then decided to circumnavigate Sicily rather than sail through the perilous Strait of Messina, watched over by Scylla, a monster whose lower half was made up of six ferocious dogs that fed on passing seafarers (on the Calabrian coast), and Charybdis, another monster who, three times a day, sucked down all that sailed on her part of the sea and devoured the hapless sailors (on the Sicilian side). Aeneas received warm welcomes from the inhabitants of the various cities and learned how other Trojan exiles, fleeing from the war, had been welcomed before them—and even that some of these, such as Aegisthus, had become the rulers of Sicilian cities. It was during this phase of the voyage that the very old and weakened Anchises died and was buried at Drepanum (Trapani) by his son Aeneas.

Dido and Aeneas

When Aeneas again put to sea his fleet was tormented by a raging storm that sent him to the coast of Africa, where he met the beautiful Phoenician queen Dido who had founded powerful Carthage. She fell in love with Aeneas and tried to convince him to remain with her as her husband, but by express order of Zeus, who could not permit Aeneas to live peacefully in a city that was destined to become the most powerful and bitter of Rome's enemies, the Trojan hero set off again toward Italy. The young and abandoned Dido was overcome by despair and killed herself on a sword; she fell on the embers of the pyre in which she had burned her mementos of Aeneas.

CVMAEA

Aeneas in Italy

When Aeneas landed at Cumae, he consulted the Cumaean Sibyl; the much-feared oracle suggested that he descend into Avernus, the local equivalent of the Greek Hades. Here Aeneas met the shades of the dead and received from them details concerning his future and those of his descendants. Back in the land of the living, Aeneas sailed on up the Italian coast, stopping to bury Ascanius's nurse Caieta, who had died on this last stage of the voyage, in the place that since then has borne her name (Gaeta). Then, after carefully skirting the island of the enchantress Circe, whose fame (especially after Odysseus' encounter with her) had spread throughout the Mediterranean, he finally came to the mouth of the Tiber. Here he debarked in the territory of Laurentum, ruled by the mythical Latinus, who welcomed the company most hospitably, offered Aeneas land on which to build a new city, and even bade him accept the hand of his daughter, Lavinia.

The Hero on the Hills of Rome

Amata, the wife of Latinus, who would have preferred that Lavinia marry Turnus, king of the neighboring and warlike Rutulians, induced him to make war against the Aeneas and his Trojan companions. But in the meantime Aeneas had left most of his men at their camp on the coast and had headed up the Tiber to the city of Pallanteum on the site of what was to become the first nucleus of Rome (Palatine), where he asked for the aid of king Evander, a Greek from Arcadia who had once been the guest of An-

Facing page, Michelangelo's monumental Cumaean Sibyl on the ceiling of the Sistine Chapel (Vatican City, Rome).

Below, warriors carrying a slain companion-at-arms. Detail of the handle of a bronze Etruscan cist. Rome, National Museum at Villa Giulia.

Bottom, the Etruscan statue of a warrior known as the Mars of Todi. Rome, Vatican Museums.

Romulus and Remus, little more than newborns, being nursed by the she-wolf against the background of an idyllic and crowded Roman landscape in a fresco by Giuseppe Cesari (1568-1640). Rome, Capitoline Museums.

The Capitoline Wolf, *a potent symbol of the Eternal City, represents a she-wolf nursing the twins Romulus and Remus. Although "born from the ashes of Troy," Roman civilization was profoundly affected by the history and culture of Greece, where myth was an essential and integral part of life.*

chises. Aeneas was welcomed and given the troops he needed, commanded by the king's own son Pallas; he then turned to the Etruscan city of Agylla (Cerveteri), where he gathered more troops. He returned to the Trojan camp just in time to turn the tide against the fierce attack launched by Turnus and the Rutulian army.

The Founding of the Eternal City

Virgil's poem closes with the death of Turnus and the victory of Aeneas; it does not, therefore, recount the subsequent events that led to the legendary founding of Rome, seen as a direct emanation of noble Troy.
According to Roman historians, Aeneas founded Lavinia and fought various of the surrounding populations to establish and consolidate his power until he died, struck down by lightning. He received public honor and worship after his death.
And while Aeneas' son Ascanius (also known as Iulus) founded the city of Albalonga, it was to a later descendent of Aeneas, Romulus, that there fell the glorious privilege of founding what was destined to become the greatest city in the world: Rome.

INDEX

Tales, Adventures, and ...

To Learn More

Neither Gods nor Heroes

On his return to Ithaca after years and years of travels, Odysseus' aged nurse recognizes the hero by an old foot wound inflicted during a boar hunt. Scene on a red-figure Attic skyphos from Chiusi, decorated by the Penelope Painter (ca. 440 BC). The scene on the other side of the vase is reproduced on page 130. Chiusi (Italy), National Archaeological Museum.

Facing page, Odysseus finally reveals himself to Penelope. Greek relief (Melian Relief) in polychrome terracotta (ca. 450 BC). Paris, Louvre.

company jeered at him; the beggar Irus, a sort of mascot to the suitors who would stop at nothing to defend his privileged position, started a fight. Odysseus dispatched the beggar and so further increased the animosity of the suitors. Still disguised, he approached Penelope and, unrecognized by her, suggested that her husband might still be alive and might even have returned to his country. But he postponed disclosure of his identity until the evening. Penelope's truce with the suitors had meanwhile come to an end, since the secret of her weaving had been revealed by one of her one servants. She had called a contest and promised that she would marry the man who succeeded in shooting an arrow through the holes in twelve axe-heads set out in a line, using the bow of Odysseus. That night, none of those assembled at the palace was able even to bend the great bow—no one except the false beggar, who bent and strung it and sent an arrow flying through the axes on his first try.

Odysseus Conquers his Kingdom

Telemachus now ordered that the palace doors be closed; the weaponless suitors were at the mercy of Odysseus and his son. Those of the servant girls who had been indiscreet were also punished: they were made to remove the bodies of the suitors felled by Odysseus and Telemachus and to wash away the blood, and then they were hanged. Only at this point did Odysseus reveal himself to his wife, allaying Penelope's doubts by disclosing details about their wedding chamber known only to themselves.

The next morning Odysseus also made himself known to his father at his country retreat. In the meantime the enraged relatives of the suitors armed themselves and set out to storm the palace, but Athena intervened in the guise of Mentor to foil their attempts at revenge. So was peace finally restored to Ithaca.